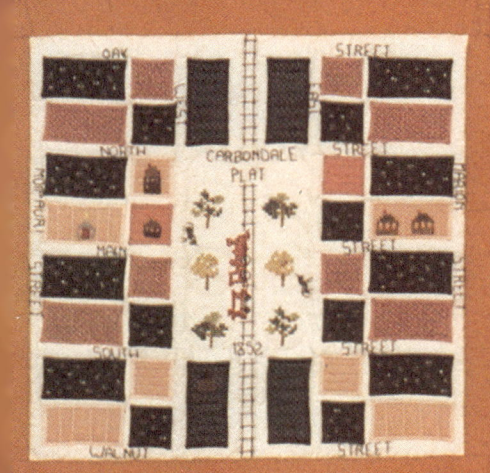

On behalf of the Board of Directors, officers and employees of First National Bank & Trust Company, we are pleased to present to our customers and friends...

**CARBONDALE: A PICTORIAL HISTORY.**

Through its pages, Carbondale's rich and vibrant history comes alive and First National Bank & Trust Company is proud to have played a vital, long-standing role in that heritage and growth.

First National Bank & Trust Company hopes this beautifully-illustrated and well-documented volume will prove a cherished addition to your family library and a valuable collectors' item in the years to come.

Charles D. Renfro
President
First National Bank and Trust

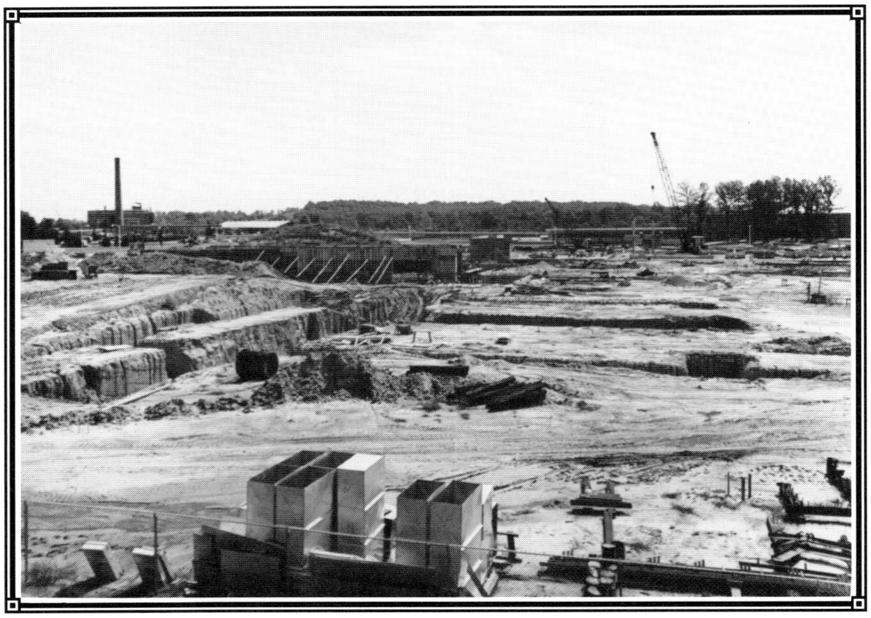

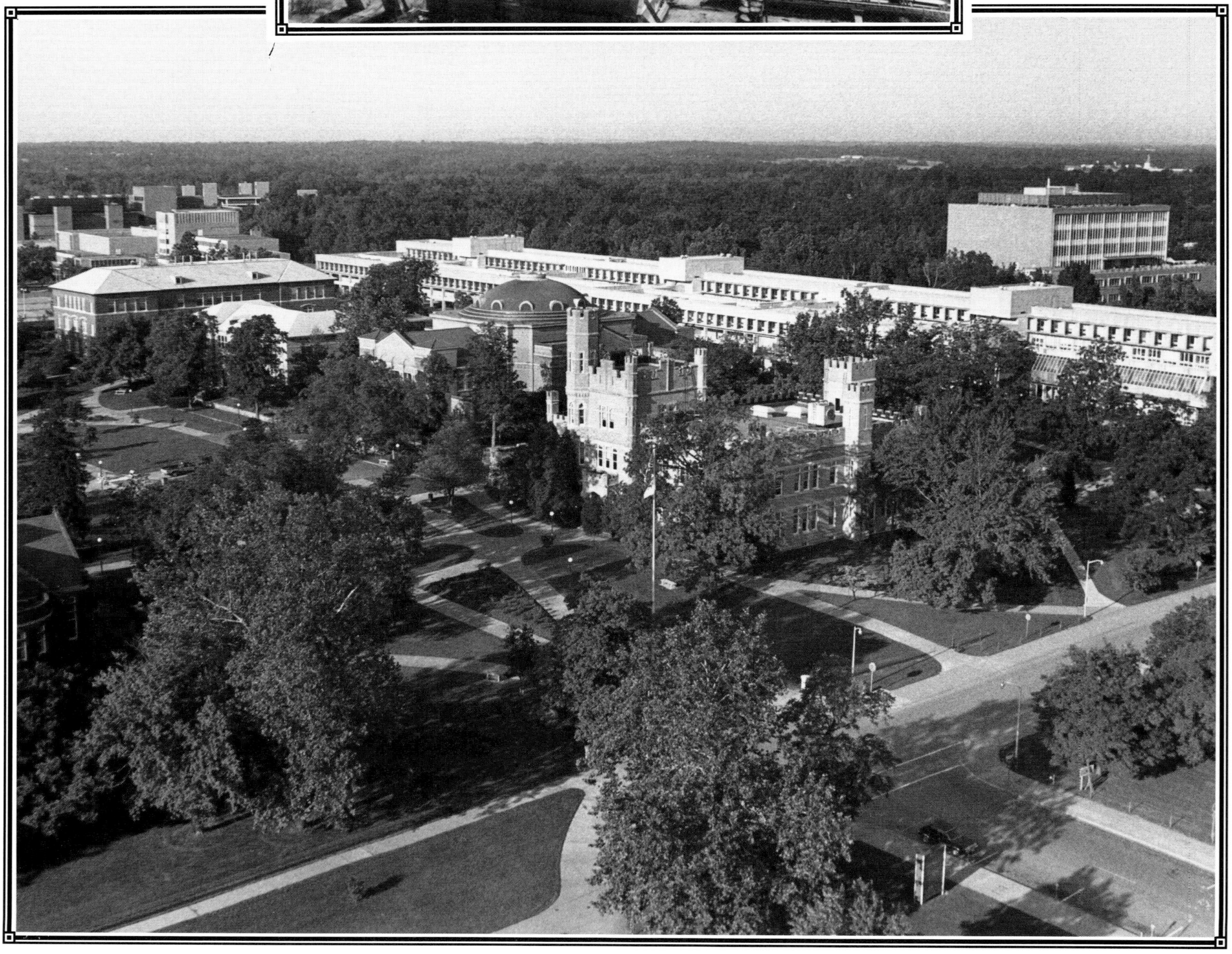

# *Carbondale*
# A Pictorial History

*by*
*Betty Mitchell*

**G. Bradley Publishing, Inc.
St. Louis, Missouri**

# Carbondale
## A PICTORIAL HISTORY

By
Betty Mitchell

A limited edition of 2,000
of which this is... 266

**Publication Staff:**
Author: Betty Mitchell
Cover Artist: Gary Butler
Book Design: Diane Kramer
Publisher: G. Bradley Publishing, Inc.
Sponsor: First National Bank and Trust Company

---

Book End Sheet Information:

### QUILT OF HISTORY OF CARBONDALE

This quilt hangs in the Carbondale Public Library. It was made by local artists, under the coordination of Millie Dunkel.

Top, left to right: *The Rapp House* — built for Frank J. Chapman in 1868, and purchased by the First Baptist Church in 1901 for use as an annex. It was demolished in 1966.

*John A. Logan* — Civil War general who was born in Murphysboro and lived for a time in Carbondale before going to Congress.

*Old Main Fire* — On June 8, 1969, (the second) Old Main on the SIU campus was burned, and was afterward razed by the Univesity.

*511 West Walnut* — built in 1858; in 1913 Dr. J. W. and Lucy Barrow sold it to Clyde L. and Mary Smith. Dr. Dan B. and Jean Smith Foley inherited it in 1964.

*First Train into Carbondale* — On July 4, 1854, the first train arrived in Carbondale on the Illinois Central Railroad, the cause for a major celebration in the town.

*Interurban* — The electric trolley that ran between Carbonale and Murphysboro in the early 1900s.

Second row, left to right: *The Roberts Hotel* — Built in 1870s by James M. Campbell and named the Newell House, the hotel was renamed the Roberts in 1903. The building remains at the corner of Main and Washington; it was remodeled in 1965 and renamed the Benning Building.

*The Illinois Central Railroad Station* — The depot was the center of the railroad activities for the town, housing the ticket office, waiting rooms, and related functions. It was built in 1904 and is currently being renovated and preserved.

*An Art Education Class* at SINU in the early 1900s; this block shows a student at the blackboard, drawing an American flag.

*Hundley House* — Originally built in 1873 at 601 West Main, this house was moved to 204 South Maple in 1917 by John C. and Luella Hundley.

*Daniel Harmon Brush* — Founder of Carbondale in 1852, he operated a general store, built the railroad freight office, helped with building the West Side School and Carbondale College, and practiced law. He died on the Brush School site, helping to remove a tree.

*Moody's Opera House* — The Opera House was on the second and third floors of the building on the northeast corner of Washington and Main Streets, currently the home of the Stage Company.

Third row, left to right: *West Side School* — a small frame building in the 400 block of West Main, built in 1856, and replaced in 1914 by Brush School, which burned on December 12, 1976. The Carbondale Public Library is on this site.

*Paul and Virginia* — the statue on the SIU campus, a gift from the class of 1887.

*Harker-Mitchell Home* — At 416 West Main, this house was built in 1868 for Judge O. A. Harker, who sold it to E. E. Mitchell in the early 1900s.

*Original City Plat* — In 1852 a survey by Dr. William Richart included 56 acres, of which 9.6 were reserved for railroad use. The surveyed area was bounded by the present streets of Oak, Walnut, University and Marion. The town was legally incorporated by the state legislature in March 1856.

*Woodlawn Cemetery* — On East Main Street, this cemetery was legally incorporated in 1854; more than sixty Civil War veterans are buried there.

*First Airport* — In early 1930s, north of Carbondale, this airport was operated by the American Legion. The plane depicted in the air is a Travelair Sport.

Bottom row: *Squirrel Tale* — based on the story that Brush replaced gray squirrels with Red Fox squirrels in Carbondale.

*Allyn House* — at 505 West Walnut, built in 1868 by Babcock and later bought by Robert Allyn, first president of SINU. Dr. J. W. Barrow bought the house in 1912; later his daughter Mary and her husband, Dr. Leo J. Brown, and their family lived in it; currently their daughter Mary Alice and her husband, Michael Kimmel, and their children live there.

*Halloween* — a publicly celebrated event in Carbondale from the early 1900s, with parades, parties, contests, and decorations.

*West Main Methodist Church* — First Methodist Church, completed in 1888, and replaced by the current building in 1922.

*"The College"* — a depiction of an early school, reportedly opened in 1832 on the Lincoln School site. It was moved to Touch of Nature at Little Grassy Lake.

*Daniel Brush Declaiming for the Union* — In 1861 Brush raised the flag on the roof of his store and spoke to the gathered crowd, supporting the Union.

---

Copyright 1991 by G. Bradley Publishing, Inc. All rights reserved. Printed in the United States of America. No part of this publication may be reproduced, stored in a retrieval system, or transmitted, in any form or by any means, electronic, mechanical, photocopying, recording or otherwise, without the prior permission of the publisher.

ISBN 0-943963-20-6
Printed in the United States of America

# TABLE OF CONTENTS

Governance .................................................................. 6

Foreword .................................................................... 7

Chapter I – Early Days: 1852-1905 ............................ 9

Chapter II – Developing: 1905-1945 ......................... 31

Chapter III – Exploding: 1945-1990 .......................... 63

Chapter IV – Public Institutions ............................... 79

Chapter V – The Illinois Central Railroad ............... 125

Chapter VI – Southern Illinois University ............... 157

Acknowledgements ................................................. 196

Contributors ............................................................ 196

Bibliography ............................................................ 197

Index ........................................................................ 198

# POPULATION AND GOVERNANCE

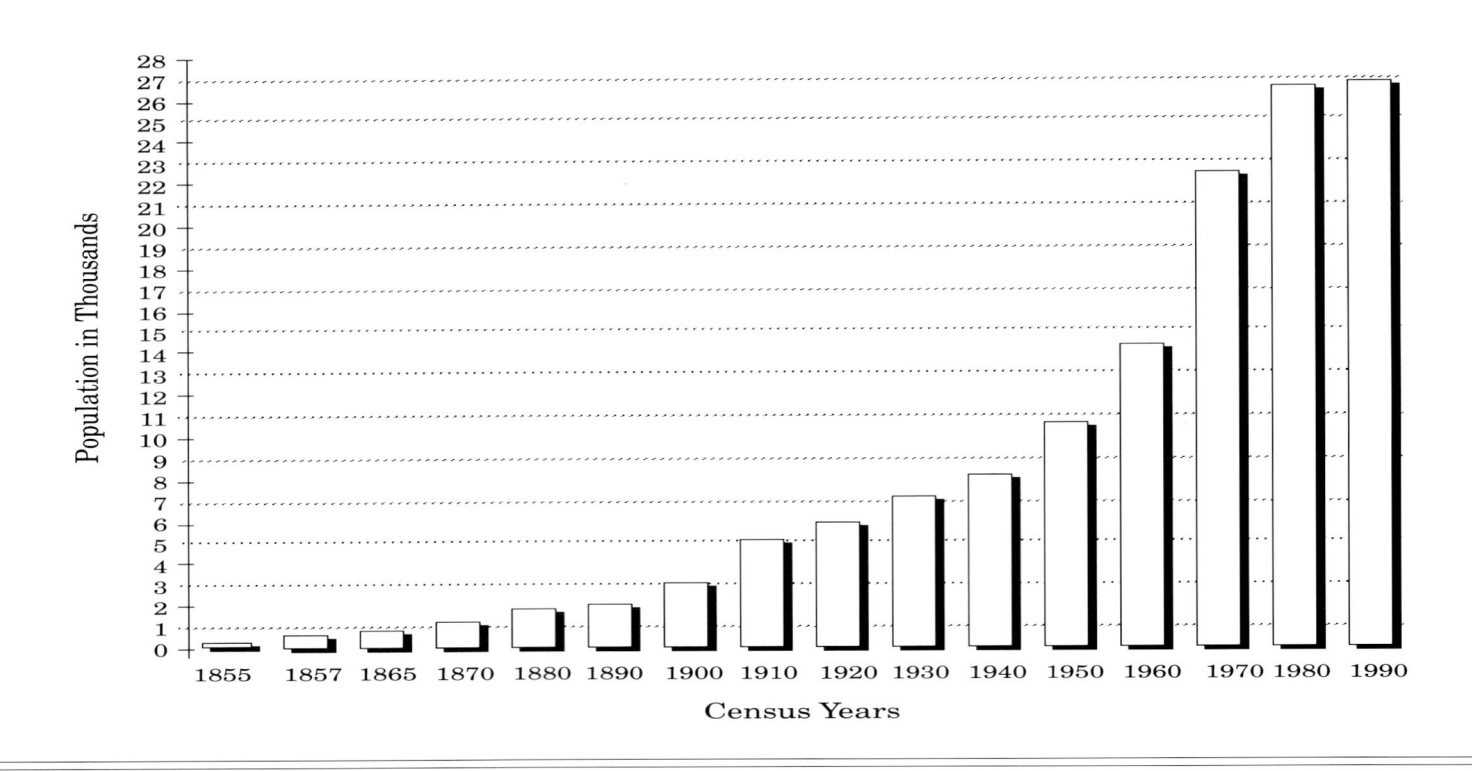

[Bar chart showing Population in Thousands by Census Years from 1855 to 1990]

---

A Board of Trustees served as the first governing body of Carbondale, from 1856 to 1869, when the mayor/council system was begun.

**Mayors:**

| | |
|---|---|
| 1868-1871 | James Boyd Richart |
| 1871 | Samuel A. Flagler (resigned) |
| 1871-1873 | James H. Crandall (replacement) |
| 1873 | A. J. Backus (died in December, 1873) |
| 1874-1876 | William Lemma |

(After 1873, Council members were designated as eldermen, each representing a ward.)

| | |
|---|---|
| 1877-1878 | F. A. Prickett |
| 1879-1886 | E. J. Ingersoll |
| 1887-1888 | J. H. Burket |
| 1889-1890 | Hugh Lauder |
| 1891-1892 | J. H. Searing |
| 1893-1894 | James M. Johnson |
| 1895-1896 | Thomas F. Hord |
| 1897-1900 | J. M. Dillinger |
| 1901-1902 | J. T. McAnally |
| 1903-1904 | Edward E. Mitchell |
| 1905-1906 | C. E. White |
| 1907-1908 | J. C. Hundley |
| 1909-1910 | C. E. White |

(On January 10, 1911, Carbondale adopted the Commission form of government. The City Clerk is appointed, not elected, in this form of government.)

| | |
|---|---|
| 1911-1914 | H. E. Curtis |
| 1915-1918 | E. K. Porter |
| 1919-1922 | F. C. Krysher |
| 1923-1926 | Bert E. Hill |
| 1927-1930 | Charles Easterly |
| 1931-1934 | J. M. Anderson |
| 1935-1938 | Leo I. Dwyer |
| 1939-1946 | Charles Johnson |
| 1947-1958 | John I. Wright |
| 1959-1966 | D. Blaney Miler |

(On September 1, 1966, C. William Norman was appointed as the first City Manager.)

| | |
|---|---|
| 1967-1970 | David Keene |

(On June 2, 1970, Norman resigned as City Manager; Carl Sisk was appointed Acting City Manager. In August 1970 William R. Schmidt was appointed City Manager.)

| | |
|---|---|
| 1971-1978 | Neal E. Eckert |

(On December 31, 1971, Schmidt resigned; William Schwegman was appointed Acting City Manager. In June, 1972, Carroll Fry was appointed City Manager.)

(On August 8, 1978, Neal Eckert resigned; Hans J. Fischer was appointed Mayor.)

| | |
|---|---|
| 1978-1982 | Hans J. Fischer |
| 1983-1986 | Helen Westberg |

(On December 1, 1983, William C. Dixon was appointed City Manager.)

| | |
|---|---|
| 1987- | Neil L. Dillard |

(On December 1, 1988, Dixon resigned. In April 1989 Steven Hoffner was appointed City Manager.)

# FOREWORD

Carbondale, often called the economic center of Southern Illinois, is located in the hills, orchards and farmlands between the confluence of the Mississippi and Ohio Rivers. Nearby are two state parks, four large lakes, and the Shawnee National Forest. Within easy reach of St. Louis, Memphis and Chicago, Carbondale also reaches out to the nearby communities, which form a commuter/feeder extension of the community.

A history of Carbondale must begin with the Illinois Central Railroad, which served as the impetus for the location in the mid-nineteenth century. The Illinois Central continued as the primary economic force from the beginning of Carbondale in 1852 until the middle of the twentieth century, when the state normal school—known as Southern Illinois State Teachers College, then as Southern Illinois Normal University, and finally as Southern Illinois University—took the role of major industry.

This pictorial history is divided into three chronological eras: from 1852 until just after the turn of the century, 1905; from 1905 to 1945; and from 1945 to the present. However, public institutions and groups (churches, schools, medical and banking facilities, recreational areas and social organizations) are treated historically within units in the fourth chapter. Then, since the role of the Illinois Central Railroad was central to the community for a century, one chapter is devoted to that role. Finally, the last chapter covers, superficially at best, the history of the University.

Although at the beginning of its history Carbondale was much like other towns on the IC Railroad and rural in atmosphere, like other towns in southern Illinois, many changes have occurred in the last four decades. Today the atmosphere is metropolitan. Governance administered by a council-manager system provides a positive approach to solving the problems created by rapid growth. Certainly life in Carbondale is ever-changing and fast moving, especially during the academic year when more than 20,000 students are in town.

Because of limited space, this history and the photographic evidence are representative, not comprehensive. Partially and realistically, the coverage is based on the available photographs. This book serves as an overview, rather than an in-depth view, of the 137 years of Carbondale history.

Daniel Harmon Brush (1813-90)

Born in Vermont, son of Ulkanah and Lucretia Harmon Brush, Brush was a resident of Jackson County and founder of Carbondale. He was a colonel in the Eighteenth Illinois Infantry in the Union Army, but he was a merchant, public official, lumberman, promoter, and lawyer. He was an active Presbyterian, and took part in the social and educational activities of Carbondale. He was accidentally killed on the Brush School grounds when a tree being cut down fell in the wrong direction and struck him. He is buried in lot number 1 of Woodlawn Cemetery which he laid out.

# CHAPTER I

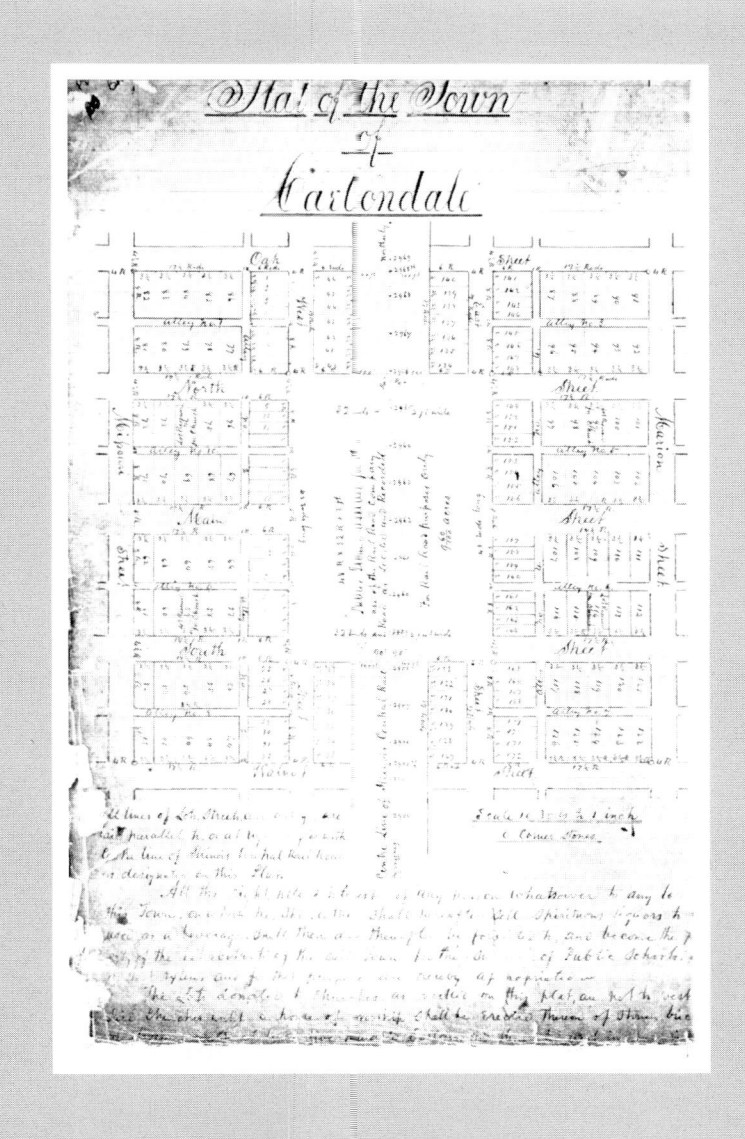

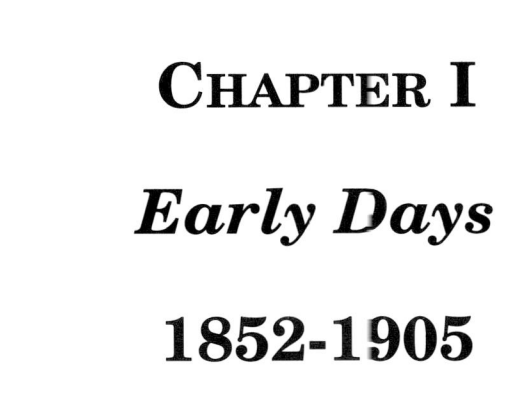

## *Early Days*

## 1852-1905

Carbondale began as a typical midwest railroad town in the mid-nineteenth century. In the summer of 1852 the Illinois Central Railroad tracks were being staked, with two proposed stations, at DeSoto and Makanda. Daniel Harmon Brush, a Murphysboro resident, miller, county official and businessman, had wanted to find an area on the new railroad to establish a town. In Brush's memoirs, he gives the following account:

*About the first of August, 1852, accompanied by Asgill Conner, I commenced my search on horseback and came to a small improvement in this vicinity owned by John Brewster. Here we were compelled to leave our horses and pick our way as best we could through a dense mass of vines, briars, and tangled underbrush until we found the line of road—a path along which was cleared of the luxuriant growth—and by the grade stakes, we could see the line of survey as well as the profile of the road, and by following the line and carefully noting the numbers on the stakes, we discovered that for about one mile, through parts of sections 16 and 21 in T 9 S R 1 W the roadbed would be level, without much excavation or filling up at any place. This level occurring in the center of an elevated and rolling scope of territory, and being likewise about midway between the points that had been apparently selected as stations, and also being nearly upon a direct line from Murphysboro to Marion, the county seat of Williamson County, struck me very forcibly as the spot I was looking for.*

*I found, moreover, that the land could be purchased at reasonable rates. Thereupon the scheme of securing ground and laying out a town here was entered into between myself and my friends, Doctor William Richart and Asgill Conner, who upon examination of the ground coincided with me in thinking the site a good one, and we agreed to move together in the project. Steps were taken to secure the land, and as we were not very flush in capital, and had an idea that we could hardly hope to secure a railway station or do much towards building up a town ourselves, it was decided that I should go to Jonesboro, then the headquarters of the railroad men, and make such arrangements as I might deem most advisable for the success of the cause. I thereupon went to Jonesboro on August 27, 1852, and made known my errand to Lewis W. Ashley, Chief Engineer of the southern division of the road. The scheme was not viewed by Mr. Ashley with much favor at first but when I signified to him the precise location of the land, he saw from his maps and surveys that the ground was favorable and that a town could be built there.*

An article of agreement was drawn up and signed by "D. H. Brush, L. W. Ashley, I. F. Ashley, A. Buck, I. Buck, Thos. Barnes, J. Dougherty, A. Conner, William Richart, H. E. Long, E. Leavenworth, and Joseph Koenig; that each contribute and pay his equal proportionate share of the purchase money required to purchase the same, not to exceed one hundred dollars each." "In pursuance of this agreement all of said lands were secured and a town was laid out on November 24, 1852. At a meeting of the proprietors, held at the office of L. W. Ashley in Jonesboro, Nov. 25, 1852, I proposed that inasmuch as the town was in a coal region it should be called Carbondale, which was agreed to, and this name was entered upon the plat. I further proposed that lots 59, 74, 99, and 114 should be reserved for donation to such churches as should first select and build thereon.... I also proposed that the sale of spiritous liquors as a beverage should be forever prohibited in the town. It was so decided by the proprietors...."

Carbondale was laid out so that all streets were parallel to or at right angles to the railroad, with a town square of 9.6 acres (the area now bordered by Jackson, Monroe, Washington, and Illinois) to be reserved for use of the railroad. Brush was given a contract to build a freight house on this location.

In December 1852 James Boyd Richart, the first mayor, built a small residence on lot 36 (215 S. Illinois). Asgill Conner built the second house in 1853 on the site now occupied by the First United Methodist Church. According to Aileen Neely's *Days of Our Years*, "While it was still an unfinished cabin, the first religious service ever held in town was held there (the Conner house) in December, 1852." Also in December 1852 on lot 17 (southwest corner of Illinois and Main) Brush built the first store, which he opened in January 1853, with Asgill Conner in charge. In September 1853 Brush set up the first steam lumber mill, at a cost of $4,000, on a site south of what is now Mill Street, because there was a small stream that would provide water in that area.

On July 4, 1854, the first major event in Carbondale was the celebration of Independence Day and the first Illinois Central train arrival, from Cairo. Stories tell that 2,000 people from the area and 500 people on the train gathered for a lunch. According to Brush:

*About noon the rumble of the train was heard, then came the shrill cry of the steam whistle, and soon the locomotive and cars slowed up and came to a stop opposite the freight house. The wonder-struck people shouted, some in terror and all in surprise. The horses cavorted and tried to break away. The dogs howled and with tails tucked between their legs stood not upon the order of their going, making hasty strides towards tall timber. The horses, scared and trembling, were mostly held in with bit and bridle, and the startled multitude, perceiving that no one was hurt, soon quieted down. A Fourth of July oration was pronounced in a grove near the station under a Union banner that I had purchased for the occasion, and the first one, I think, ever hoisted in the county.*
\* \* \*
*I had laid in a lot of skyrockets, Roman candles, torpedoes, firecrackers, magic wheels, wriggling serpents, etc., and had announced that when night came a display of fireworks would be made, and invited all who desired to remain and see the sight.... The magic*

*wheels rolled and tumbled, the Roman candles shot forth the best they could, the crackers all popped at once, and the torpedoes with loud reports exploded.*

*The scene was highly animated and exciting while it lasted, and brought forth yells of delight from the beholders. Soon, however, perceiving that most of the persons present considered the denouement legitimate, and as designed, I let the matter go without explanation.*

In the late 1850s Carbondale developed slowly, but churches, schools, and a variety of stores and businesses existed: dry goods, drug, grocery, hardware and furniture stores, blacksmith shops, a livery stable, a hotel, a printing office, and steam-powered flour and saw mills. In 1856 the West Side School and, in the late 1850s, the East Side School were built. Another, Carbondale College, was planned in 1856 but not completed until the 1860s, at the site of the present Lincoln School. The hotel, Planters House, was at 200 North Illinois. According to the Illinois State Census, in 1855, 241 people were living in Carbondale, but by 1865, the number had grown to 1,030.

John A. Logan, who had moved to Carbondale in 1861, recruited the Thirty-first Regiment of Illinois Infantry. Of the 250 Carbondale men who enlisted in the Civil War, 55 or more were killed. On April 29, 1866, at Woodlawn Cemetary the first memorial services—in Illinois and perhaps in the country—marked the burial of those killed. According to Wright, "When this day came, a group of more than 200 veterans from the area gathered at the Old Blue Church on East Jackson Street, where Methodist minister J. W. Lane was waiting to greet them. The marshals of the day, Col. E. J. Ingersoll and Col. Daniel H. Brush, mounted their horses to lead the parade to Woodlawn Cemetery. Arrived there, the Reverend Lane led the assemblage in prayer. Gen. John A. Logan, their fellow-townsman, made the principal speech, striking the theme: 'Every man's life belongs to his country, and no man has a right to refuse when the country calls for it.'" Wright goes on, "Logan was impressed by the observance, which was repeated the next year, and as commander of the Grand Army of the Republic, on May 5, 1868, he signed General Order No. 11, setting May 30, 1868, as a Memorial Day, which it was hoped would be 'kept up from year to year.' By 1888 it had been made a legal holiday in twelve northern states. Later it became recognized as a legal holiday throughout the country."

In the period after the Civil War, Carbondale prospered—after a slow beginning—with building both businesses and homes. Wright comments, "The so-called Panic of 1873 was primarily a money panic, and for this reason, since Carbondale did not have any large financial institution to be adversely affected by the money shortage, the city escaped the worst of the effects of the economic situation . . . . As a fairly new community whose normal development had been arrested during the Civil War years, the postwar boom period lasted much longer for Carbondale than it did for some communities. . . . Another boost for Carbondale's economy during this period came from its increasing importance as a transportation center, due to its location on the Illinois Central line."

Serious discussions of a new state teachers college in 1868 led to much competition among southern Illinois towns. On August 31, 1869, Carbondale was chosen, primarily because of its geographic location (about the center of the area), its railroad, and its temperance. Although the cornerstone was laid on May 17, 1870, completion and occupation was not until July 1, 1874. The building activity at the end of Missouri Avenue (re-named Normal) also contributed to the prosperity of the community. Maycock sums up this period, "From the time construction really began [of the new normal school] until the building's destruction [it burned] in 1883, the city passed through a period of optimism and commercial expansion in the early 1870s, suffered the effects of a severe nation wide depression in 1873 and railroad strikes in 1877, and finally achieved a renewal of growth and business activity in the early 1880s." At any rate, construction of new homes, many of them quite large, increased in the 1880s.

Throughout this period a number of newspapers had begun but not prospered: in 1857-58, the *Carbondale Transcript*; in 1859, the *Times*, which was sold in 1864 and changed to *New Era* and then to *Carbondale Observer*; in 1877, sold again and changed to *Carbondale Free Press*. Another, the *Carbondale Democrat* sprung up in 1876 but did not survive. In the early 1890s a number of amateur newspapers originated, including *Our Sanctum* (1893) and *The Observer* (1897), both published by Charles Duncan Miller Renfro I.

Another depression in 1893 resulted in what Wright calls "a blessing in disguise" because it led to the establishment of the First National Bank. According to Wright, "This was the result of the action of a group of Carbondale businessmen who seized the opportunity and converted the disaster into a benefit for the citizens of Carbondale. Frank A. Prickett, whose drugstore had been in the Richart and Campbell building, was one of the leaders of the group. The First National Bank was chartered under the laws of the state of Illinois on May 25, 1893, with a capital of $50,000, all paid up. Prickett became president of the bank and William A. (Gus) Schwartz, vice president." By 1905 Gus Schwartz was president, Judge O. A. Harker vice president, E. E. Mitchell, cashier, W. H. Ashley, assistant cashier, and J. E. Mitchell, teller. Directors were Schwartz, Harker, J. D. Peters, E. E. Mitchell, and J. C. Hundley.

The second floor of the bank building was occupied

by the opera house, which existed in 1887 and probably before that. It seated 600. The December 10, 1887, program of the Zetetic and Socratic Societies (undergraduate clubs at the Normal), tells that it was called Moody's Opera House.

On June 11, 1891, the first electricity was supplied by the Carbondale Electric Company, which in 1892 sunk artesian wells to augment the water supply from Thompson's Lake. By 1896, Carbondale boasted five hotels: the Edwards House (northwest corner of Illinois and Jackson), the Southern Hotel (on West Jackson), the Newell House (southeast corner of Main and Washington), the Hundley House (on Main Street), and the East Side Hotel (on South Washington). Since the city opted for saloons in the election of 1895, there were four in 1896, although the decision was reversed and then reversed back again in 1899. In addition, the number of other businesses had expanded to include photographers, a tailor, shoe shops, a harness shop, a public laundry, a book store, and three jewelers. Carbondale was growing, as the census figures reveal 2,382 in 1890 and 3,318 in 1900.

The period immediately following the turn of the century saw a rapid expansion of the population. By 1905 the population was almost 5,000, probably the result of two factors, the expansion of the railroad and in 1903 the beginning of the Ayer and Lord Tie Company, the largest railroad-tie plant in the country with an annual payroll of $85,000. By 1900 the city had mail delivery, by 1902 a city sewer system, and by 1903, the first daily newspaper, the *Daily Free Press*.

According to Maycock, "the commercial activity and particularly retail sales continued to concentrate on the public square." ". . . of the two hundred firms listed in the business directory in 1905, all but fifteen were located along Main Street or around the square." The integrity of the square was broken, however, when the city council in March 1903 vacated West Monroe Street, to accommodate the new railroad depot (which had been on the east side of the tracks).

---

Left: Carbondale's public square has been its focal point and center of gravity since the city was founded in 1852. Yet it was always the domain of the railroad and, as such, was never properly utilized by the community. This 1870 photograph, looking toward the northeast, shows the first generation of downtown buildings, mostly of wood. The building at the far left housed *The New Era*, the city's first real newspaper.

Batson's Livery and Boarding Stable. Evidence of a variety of Batsons exists, but, except for this picture, there is no information on the location of Batson's Livery Stable.

Planters House Hotel, at 200 North Illinois Avenue, was originally called the Union House, one of several hotels built around the town square in the early days of the community to serve the railroad business as well as farmers and traders calling on Carbondale merchants. The building, which dates from 1858, was later changed to the Franklin Hotel. It was razed in 1991.

12

The southwest corner of the square in 1866, opposite the New Hundley Hotel. The Borger Building was on the corner of South Illinois and Monroe Streets.

North Illinois at Jackson, looking south. The building on the corner began as Oldenhage and Fakes Saloon, now restored as the Oldenhage and Hughes building.

# John A. Logan

General John A. Logan (1826-1886)

Born in Murphysboro, General Logan moved with his family to Carbondale, where they lived from 1861 to 1871, at 400 West Oak, which was lot 452, a little more than an acre that extended from Oak to Pecan, with Pine Street on the east. He was commander in chief of the Grand Army of the Republic in the Civil War. When he was elected to the Senate in 1871, he moved to Chicago.

General Logan's Home

**Woodlawn Cemetery**

Woodlawn Cemetery was incorporated by a special act of the legislature in 1854, two years before the town was incorporated. Over 60 Civil War veterans were buried there, at least 20 of them during the war. It is operated by the Carbondale Cemetery Association.

Photographer Robert "Rip" Stokes is credited for finding this photograph of Ingersoll and his men.

Col. Ingersoll's house at 411 West Main

**Col. Ezekiel James Ingersoll (1836-1925)**

Born in Indiana, Ingersoll moved to Carbondale in 1859 and opened a clock repair and jewelry store in the Campbell building (southeast corner of Main and Washington). In July 1862 he enlisted in Company H, Seventy-third Illinois Infantry. After the war he returned to his business, Ingersoll and Sheppard.

# People

Samuel W. Dunaway (1841-1905)

Dunaway, a real estate dealer, came to Carbondale in the 1870s. The house he built and lived in at 409 West Main was bought in 1919 by Dr. Moss and later by Burnett Shryock. It still stands and is known as the Muckelroy Apartments. Shryock added the front entrance doors, which he moved from the old Baptist Church on East Jackson Street.

Andrew D. Duff (1820-1889)

Duff was the eleventh child of Philip and Mary Duncan Duff, who moved to Illinois in 1809. By 1842 he taught school and began in 1846 to read law. After two years in the Mexican War he finished his law and was made county judge in Franklin County in 1849, was admitted to the bar in 1850, was named judge of the 26th judicial circuit, was a member of the 1862 Illinois constitutional convention, was reelected to circuit judge in 1867, and moved to Carbondale in 1873. He married Mary E. Powell; they had four children; the family lived at 332 West Oak. In the 1896 Carbondale city directory he was listed as a merchant; he served as Carbondale alderman in 1892 and 1893.

Richard T. Lightfoot was the son of R. P. Lightfoot (1828-1889), a physician who brought his family to Carbondale in the 1870s. His father was known for making house calls in any kind of weather. In 1880 Dr. Lightfoot built his home at 520 University. The house was sold to Eli G. Lentz in 1919. Richard Lightfoot's brother, Henry (1860-1919), became a doctor and, according to the 1905 Carbondale city directory, lived in the family home with his family. Henry served as a Carbondale alderman in 1899.

Richard T. Lightfoot (1864-?)

Daniel Baldwin Parkinson (1845-1923)
Having graduated from McKendree College in 1868, plus a year of graduate study at Northwestern University, Parkinson came to Carbondale as a member of the first faculty at the Normal School. In 1896 he lived at 335 West Walnut, and then he moved to the corner of Walnut and Poplar (now the site of the St. Francis Xavier Catholic Church). In 1892 he was named registrar and vice regent of the university and became president in 1897, an office he retained until he retired in 1913.

Eustis Patten (1845-1927)
Patten came to Carbondale in 1865, married Jessie Brainard, and they had three children, Arthur E., Edward S., and Lucy M. He first worked for a druggist, William Storer, and eventually owned the firm. Jessie Patten died in 1885, and he married Josephine Coughanour in 1886. Three druggists who began under him were E. K. Porter, Claude Fox, and F. M. Hewitt. In 1878 he built a home at what was then 800 West Main. (It is now numbered 808.) He was a continuous member of the Carbondale Baptist Church from 1869. His daughter Lucy married Dr. James W. Barrow (parents of Mary Barrow Brown, wife of Dr. Leo J. Brown).

McAnally's father, John F., became a doctor in Tennessee and moved his family to Carbondale in the 1870s. His son, John T., taught for three years before he became a physician. In the late 1880s he married Winona Pace. He shared an office on the second floor of the Patten drugstore building (corner of Main and Illinois) with Dr. H. C. Mitchell. He lived at 118 West Main. He served as president of the Southern Illinois Medical Association and in 1903 of the state medical group. He was alderman of the first ward in 1897, and in 1901 was elected mayor. In 1905 he was living at 307 West Main.

John Thomas McAnally (1857-1913)

# Homes

511 West Walnut

The oldest known house in existence in Carbondale, the original part was built for John Brewster in 1858; it consisted of a narrow hall through the center with two rooms on both sides. It has been added on to both sides. Photo taken 1918.

511 West Walnut—Interior

520 South University

Built for Dr. Lightfoot, 1884-85, this house still stands. For students at the university in the twenties-thirties-forties, it was known as Dean Lentz' house.

417 West Main

On the southeast corner of Poplar and Main, this house was built for Henry Campbell in 1882. The architect was Charles Brush. The house burned in 1896 and was replaced by the structure currently there by W. H. Phillips in 1901. The Campbell house introduced a restraint to the Victorian influence that had been exhibited in some of the early houses.

601 West Main

On the southwest corner of Maple and Main, this house was built for G. T. Winne, a real estate dealer, in 1873. In 1915 J. C. Hundley bought it and moved it to 204 South Maple, where it stands today.

# HOMES

**409 West Main**

Built for Samuel Dunaway in 1881, this house represents the typical ornate style of the Victorians. It still stands and is known as the Muckelroy Apartments.

**West of Carbondale**

This old home on the old Murphysboro Road belonged to J. C. Hundley. Ca. 1890s.

South Illinois

Listed as the corner of Freeman and Illinois, this house was Dr. McAnally's before he built on West Main Street.

401 West Walnut

Built in 1887-88 for Professor Daniel Parkinson, who had lived at 804 South Illinois before he became president of the university in 1897. The largest on Walnut at the time, and praised for its lavish interior, the house cost $3,500. Later it became the home of Charles Feirich, and in 1956 it was demolished to make way for the St. Francis Xavier Church.

Sunday Gathering

On the front porch are Frances Smith, Mrs. G. W. Smith, Professor G. W. Smith, Mrs. D. B. Parkinson, Dr. D. B. Parkinson, Alice Parkinson, Merian McAnally, Mrs. McAnally, Dr. John T. McAnally, Clyde Smith, Lawrence Harrington, Raymond Parkinson.

# HOMES

**209 West Elm**

Built about 1865 for Judge Duff. The Millers lived here for years, and in 1952 the Williams.

**808 West Main**

Built in 1878, at what was then 800 West Main, for Eustis Patten, this house still stands, though it has been changed considerably.

509 West Walnut (top photo)

E. E. Mitchell came to Carbondale in 1893 and was a cashier at the First National Bank. In 1897 he built this house, which burned in 1921. E. E. Mitchell's daughter was Julia Mitchell Etherton, who wrote about it: "It had a wide entrance hall with an oak stairway. There were four rooms downstairs; two fireplaces with mirrored oak mantels and a large bay window. Its cushioned window seat was a favorite play center. There were five bedrooms upstairs and a large attic where we played on rainy days. In the attic was a huge water tank that was filled by a rubber hose that led from two deep cisterns and was pumped full by a faithful colored man named Price. Carbondale had no water works then, so by this system we had a bathroom with modern plumbing fixtures. The yard had beautiful oak trees and trumpet vines with orange colored blossoms. . . . A rope swing hung from a high limb of the black oak on the west, and under the white oak on the east were two big stones on which we cracked hickory nuts or black walnuts for fudge or brownies. . . . I had a happy, carefree childhood with my brother and three sisters and the children on Walnut Street. We looked forward to the 4th of July celebrations."

416 West Main (middle photo)

In 1906 E. E. Mitchell bought this house, which was built in 1868, from Judge Oliver Harker, who became Dean of the Law School at the University of Illinois. Julia Mitchell Etherton writes of it, "My three sisters and I were all married in this home, before the marble mantel in the back parlor. I loved the parties and the big family gatherings. On a cold winter day we would pop corn by the library fire. We made fudge and pulled taffy and molasses candy. Often in winter evenings our father read aloud from "The Lady of the Lake" or Ernest Seton Thompson's wonderful stories, while mother sat sewing or mending. It was a beautiful street to us in any season, inches deep in dust or ankle deep in mud. Sometimes in winter it looked like a crystal forest. The summer they put in the first brick pavement we waded in the white sand and pretended we were at the seashore. When they started to lay the bricks my father turned the hose on them at night; those that soaked up water he threw out. He and the contractor exchanged letters by American Express; they were too hot for the mails to handle. We finally got our new pavement."

Kindergarten class of Julia Mitchell Etherton.

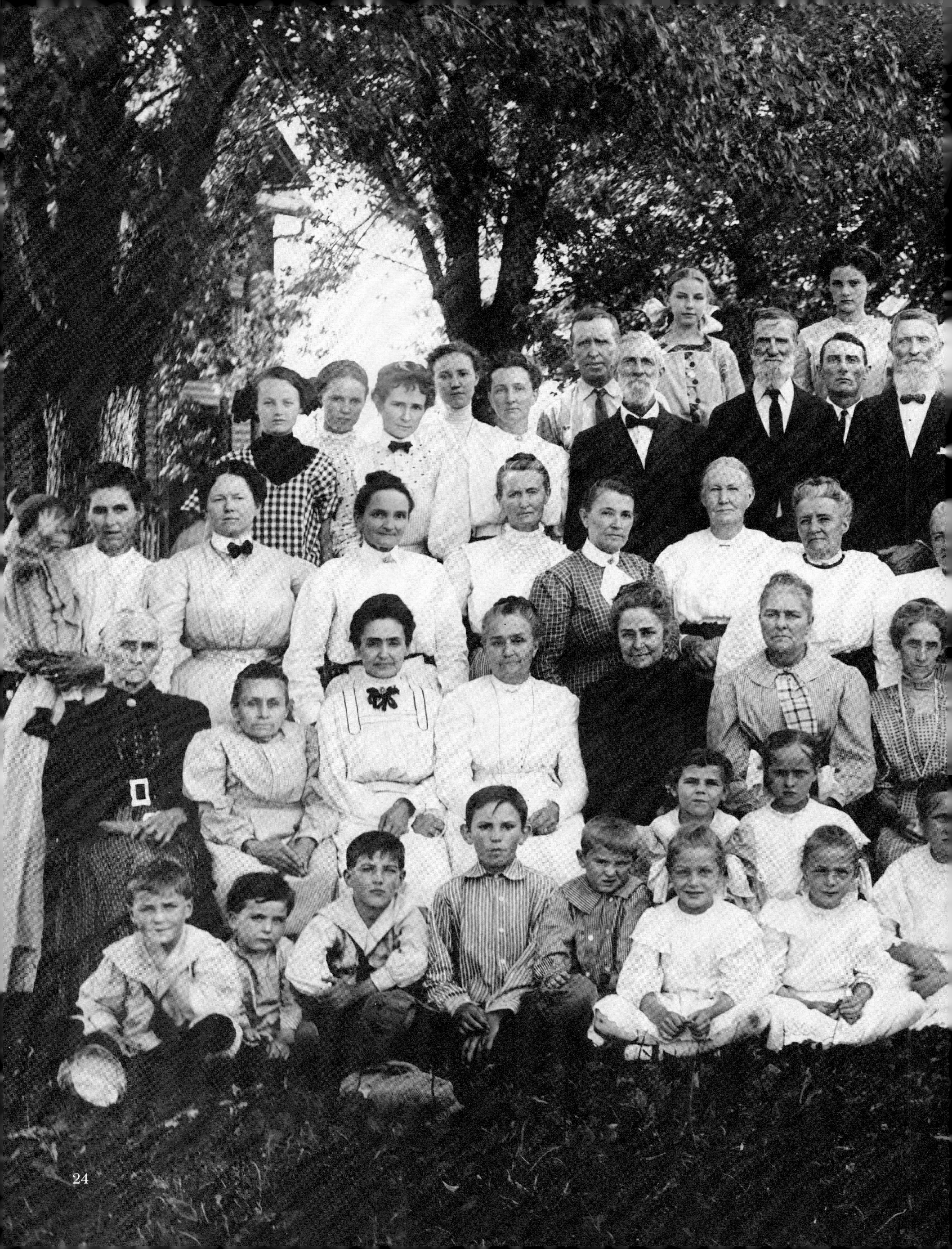

The Schwartz Family, ca. 1905. Probably the families of the Kimmels, Copelands, and Hayses are also included here, but the photo represents the typical family reunion, when all had to remain still while the photographer took the picture. Sarah Kimmel Schwartz, mother of William "Gus" Schwartz, is holding a framed picture of George Schwartz, father of William.

# EARLY BUSINESSES

South Illinois Avenue (100 block)

Looking north from Illinois Avenue and Monroe Street around the turn of the century, the viewer can see well-kept dirt streets, perhaps carefully manicured for the camera man. In the background, at the northeast corner of Jackson and Illinois can be seen the turret of the Soloman and Winters store. There are no known detailed photographs of the building. The railroad's water tower shown at right was demolished around 1940. During the 30s and early 40s Carbondale's possibly most magnificent vehicle, a scarlet and gold Model T popcorn wagon, stood on the corner at the left. Note the caption refers to West Street, the original title for Illinois Avenue.

South Illinois Avenue (100 block)

An earlier view of the same block.

North Illinois Avenue (100 block)

The building at 100 North Illinois is the only one of the four early buildings on the main street corners to have been replaced. Toward the end of the 1800s, both a bank and Patten's drugstore shared space. When the druggist retired in 1906, the bank expanded to fill the entire first floor. It was demolished and replaced by the present structure in 1928.

South Illinois Avenue (100 block)

From Main Street looking south, this view shows The New Brush Building at the corner, and to its left, the Brush Building. The corner structure, completed in 1895, replaced Carbondale's first commercial building, the wooden general store erected by city founder Daniel Brush in 1852. The building is largely intact today, although the first story facade has been superficially altered. The 100 block of South Illinois is the only commercial block in Carbondale to retain all of its turn-of-the-century second generation buildings.

**Postal Carrier**
John Logan Golliher (1852-1925) was a rural mail carrier for Route #2, Carbondale, for fifteen years, from 1901-1915. This photograph was taken before paved streets at the intersection of Jackson and Washington. Golliher married Isadora Greathouse in 1875; they had thirteen children, of whom four survived: Willard, John, Dallas, and Emma Golliher Miller.

**Main and Washington**
The northeast corner of Main and Washington, this structure housed the Prickett and Porter Drug Store and the First National Bank on the first floor, as well as the Opera House on the second and third floors.

28

New Hundley Hotel

Opened for business in November, 1899, the New Hundley Hotel boasted two upper floors that contained thirty-three rooms plus parlors. Since the building was L-shaped, it allowed every room to be on an outside wall with good light and ventilation. Standing on the balcony are Charles Hundley (in the light suit) and Mrs. Hundley. It was on the southeast corner of Monroe and Illinois.

North Illinois Avenue (100 block)

Looking south from Jackson Street, two well-known businesses on the square were the Oldenhage and Fakes Saloon and The Leader.

W. Arthur "Big Boy" Parrish (1882-1945) operated his milk delivery business, in the vicinity of Walnut Street, delivering raw milk to the households there. The business, Carbondale Everyday Diary, was the predecessor of the New Era Diary, which Parrish ran with his sons, Kenneth ("Shorty"), Bill, and Gordan.

Modern Woodmen

These Modern Woodmen, each equipped with a ceremonial axe, muster at Illinois Avenue and Main Street about 1900. In the background is the First Methodist Church tower, after its tall steeple was removed.

# CHAPTER II

*Development*

**1905-1945**

The period of 1905 to 1945 saw Carbondale through two major wars and a depression. By 1910 the census shows a jump to 5,411, and the population continued to climb steadily in this period: in 1920, to 6,267; in 1930, to 7,528; and in 1940, to 8,550. In the ten years prior to World War I, according to Maycock, "... Carbondale experienced a period of intense public building, as the city sought to provide services and facilities appropriate to its rapid growth since the turn of the century. During these years Carbondale constructed its first city hall (1914) and hospital (1912), greatly extended its sewer system (1913), and replaced its early wooden schools with modern brick structures (1914). A large-scale effort to pave its streets with brick and concrete began in 1911, and in 1912 the city voted to macadamize the roads leading into town as part of a statewide hard roads campaign. [According to Dr. Leo J. Brown, the first streets were paved by Barney Craine of paving bricks made by the Murphysboro Egyptian Brick Company.] A final indication of Carbondale's growth was the interurban electric railway to Murphysboro that had been planned as early as 1899 but actually opened in 1917."

Social and cultural activities further enhanced the city. The Elks Club was built in 1914-15 at 220 West Jackson Street, where it still serves its members. The Masons, who had occupied an upper floor in the old brick building on the northwest corner of Main and Illinois, contributed to the three-story city hall on the northwest corner of Marion and West Main, in an unusual arrangement, allowing them use of the third floor. Social clubs formed by the women included the Home Culture Club and the Philomathean Literary Society.

Mostly life in Carbondale in these years was pastoral, with barns in back yards to accommodate a cow, some chickens, and a garden. Although there were three movie houses, people created their own leisure activities, which included parades on July 4 and Halloween, and simple pleasures, such as going to Giant City. Children found fun in swinging, playing in the dirt, or the rain barrel (a commonplace part of most households, used to catch soft rain water for special purposes).

The automobile brought a change in life style to those who could afford it, enabling them to take short trips to nearby communities. A news item in the *Herald* in 1910 notes that "Messrs. G. R. Huffman, T. B. F. Smith, Claude Dixon and Bert E. Hill attended the public installation of Knights of Pythias lodge at DeSoto Monday evening, making the trip in the Huffman auto. Although the trip was made after dark, the auto performed perfecly [sic]."

By 1913 commercial activities were extended down South Illinois Avenue, and the public square received a smaller amount of interest. The residential building increased. According to Maycock, "From 1913 until the First World War, Carbondale also experienced a boom in residential building, as the demand for housing, and particularly rental housing, far outstripped the supply. Local contractors and carpenters were pressed to the limits, and additional laborers had to be imported from neighboring towns. In spite of this activity, few new subdivisions were laid out in this period. Many lots platted in the previous decade were still available, particularly in the northwest where Oakland Heights remained largely undeveloped. Much of this area remained quite rural in character as late as 1916 when a twelve-acre farm was still functioning on Bridge Street near Oakland Heights."

World War I had the usual impact (casualties are listed on plaques in the foyer of Shryock Auditorium), and in 1918 the flu epidemic struck, but construction increased significantly after the war. In the early 1920s the city's boundaries expanded considerably, with subdivisions, bungalow construction, and a new high school counting for most of the effort. One of the largest subdivisions was the 1924 Community Addition, encompassing the area from Chestnut to Rigdon streets and from the railroad to Bridge Street. But there were smaller developments in Oakland Heights, Whitney Heights, and in the area from Chautauqua to Mill streets. In addition, Maycock reports, "The need for housing also encouraged adventurous developers to move into new areas west of Oakland Avenue between Main and Sycamore streets and east of Wall Street near the tie plant. A 1924 subdivision known as Tie Plant Place created over two hundred standard building lots and numerous new streets between Wall Street and the railroad north of Fisher Street, indicating the continued importance of Ayer and Lord in developing the northeast."

The 1920s also saw increased commercial activities, which included the new Good Luck Glove Factory on College and Washington as well as new automobile garages and filling stations. According to Maycock, "In 1903 there was only one automobile in Carbondale. By 1923 Jackson County had one car for every thirteen residents, and hard roads passed through Carbondale in all directions. By 1927 the number of cars had so reduced traffic on the electric railway between Carbondale and Murphysboro that service was abandoned and the equipment sold for scrap." The old Keeley Institute was remodeled into the Amy Lewis Hospital in 1922. In 1926 E. W. Vogler established a $100,000 Ford agency, at 301 North Illinois, where there had been a flour mill. The new building for the Carbondale National Bank was built in 1928 at the corner of Illinois and Main. In 1925 Carbondale was a relief center when the tornado hit the area. The first airfield opened in 1928, north of town.

Although the Great Depression took its toll on Carbondale, the banks remained open, and both the railroad and the university continued to give employment and business to the Carbondale community. In addition, the Carbondale Business Men's Association (organized in 1903 with various name changes) contributed to the economy in the early 1930s: in 1931 it is credited for bringing to Carbondale the Kroger warehouse and division office, the American Pants Factory from Hillsboro to occupy the old Marx Haas garment factory building on East Main Street (later became the Lerner-Sloane Clothing Corporation), and in 1933 the Baptist Book Store (the Illinois Baptist State Association built a building at 306 West Main later). In 1935 the Producers Creamery occupied a North Illinois Avenue building that the Association had raised funds for and built in 1927 for the Menzie Shoe Company, which did not come to Carbondale. The Association is also credited for helping to secure the Armory and the Illinois State Health Laboratory (the Association paid $1500 toward the site). The Kroger Company at 600 North Illinois provided a payroll of over $500 a day, according to the *Herald* (January 9, 1934). Little new construction took place, however, with some exceptions: financed outside of Carbondale were the U.S. Post Office at 301 West Main in 1931 and the Illinois National Guard Armory at 900 West Sycamore in 1937. Carbondale profited from the federal efforts to ease the depression through two major work forces, the WPA and the CCC. The WPA paved a number of streets, including Elm, and built the "new gym" at CCHS on Springer in 1933, McAndrew Stadium at the University in 1938, and the Illinois State Health Laboratory on the corner of Chautauqua and Oakland in 1940-41.

According to the *Herald* (June 1, 1937), Crab Orchard Lake—contributed primarily to the foresight and efforts of Kent Keller, Congressman of Twenty-fifth Illinois District, from Ava, Illinois—was just beginning. The headline read, "Constructing Dam for Crab Orchard Lake—First Dirt Is Moved Wednesday." The article reported, "Despite sarcasm from envious sources, and efforts to ridicule the project, actual work on the Crab Orchard reservoir dam was started on Wednesday of this week, and on Friday the work of clearing the site for the spillway was started." Details of the U.S. government's buying the land followed. During the war it served a dual function: as recreation and as a source of water for the munitions plant.

Construction of the Varsity Theater in 1940 at 418 South Illinois encouraged more commercial ventures on that end of the street, including a bus depot across the street from the Varsity (at 411 and 417 South Illinois) and a brick building built for the City Dairy in 1942 (at 521 South Illinois). World War II halted further development of the town, but life during the war continued at its usual pace.

In the war years the Illinois Central moved extra people to Carbondale to keep the railroad staffed. The depot was a dynamic place 24 hours a day. Some nearby restaurants, such as the Ritz Cafe in the 200 block of South Illinois, remained open all night. Three hotels—the Franklin (Jackson and Illinois), the Roberts (Main and Washington), and the Prince (Monroe and Illinois)—served the passengers. Traffic on the rails continued to be busy into the early 50s; an estimated 28 passenger trains plus the freight trains passed through Carbondale on a daily basis.

In 1941 the Illinois Highway office building was built on Illinois 13 west of town (the office had orginally come to Carbondale in 1917). The state highway west of town (Illinois 13) was on West Sycamore Street, while Route 51 south of town followed Normal Avenue to Grand, went west on Grand one block (around the campus), and then south on Thompson Street, past the University Cafeteria (corner of Chautauqua and Thompson) and a number of residences.

This photo of Elizabeth Harris Lewis and Mary Marberry Swindell was taken in 1913 on unpaved South Popular Street.

33

The front of G. R. Huffman's store at 112 South Illinois, ca. 1901.

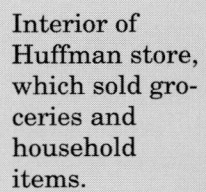

Interior of Huffman store, which sold groceries and household items.

One of the first three cars in Carbondale, this belonged to G. R. Huffman. Seated are the Huffman children, Ana, Nyle, Bernice, Gladys, and Otis, with G. R. Huffman, ca. 1908.

The Huffman Furniture and Undertaking delivery truck. In it are Ana and Pauline Huffman, ca. 1913.

South Illinois Avenue, looking toward Main and Jackson. Note the stop sign in the intersection. The building on the right, housing the cleaning business, was the Prince Hotel, later demolished.

210 West Oak, the Huffman Funeral Home was originally built in 1925; the west wing was added in 1952.

# Scrapbook

Jean Smith Foley in 1912, pulling a cart.

Mary Powers Smith in 1911 behind houses on Walnut Street. (Elm Street did not exist.)

Mary Powers Smith and Helen Smith in 1911 at 605 West Walnut.

1910 at 605 West Walnut, left to right, Clyde L. Smith, Frank Easterly, two unknown, Helen Smith, and remainder unknown.

An alternative to the horse and buggy, one of the many brands of automobiles in 1911.

In 1936, Kent Keller was a candidate for U.S. Congress.

37

# Homes

505 West Walnut. Described by Maycock as "The earliest Bracketed-Italianate building surviving in Carbondale . . . , begun in 1868 for Edwin Babcock, a schoolteacher who had married the daughter of one of the town's wealthy early settlers. As originally constructed, the house was only two stories high, with a low hip roof, segmental arched windows, and handsome scrolled brackets under the wide projecting eaves." The History of Shekinah Lodge No. 241 adds that "This home was built by Isaac Rapp. . . . It was later occupied by Brother Boyd. . . ." Boyd had bought it in 1870 for $5,500. Dr. Robert Allyn, first president of SINU, bought it in 1879 for $3,000 and added the mansard roof, the bay window, the one-story wing to the west, and a glass conservatory at the back. The house had a cistern and two wells, which had water cool enough to chill the milk. Allyn and his heirs kept the house until after the turn of the century, when it was used as a rooming house for men working on the railroad. In 1910 Dr. James W. Barrow, who was living at 511 West Walnut, bought it and lived in it until 1948, when his son-in-law Dr. Leo Brown bought it and moved his family there.

E. K. Porter (1860-1937)

Born in Salem, Illinois, and a schoolmate and friend of William Jennings Bryan, Porter graduated from the University of Illinois in 1885 and came to Carbondale to work in Eustis Patten's drug store. He clerked there until 1892, when he bought half interest in Frank A. Prickett's drug store. In 1900 he became sole owner of the Prickett and Porter Drug Store, which was at 101 North Washington. In 1919 he sold the store to Claude Fox, who moved it to the Dickerman Building (northwest corner of Walnut and Illinois) in 1925. Porter recalled the time when wheat wagons lined up as far east as Westlawn Cemetery, waiting to ship on the railroad. When he was on the school board in 1901, he noted that the superintendent, O. E. Harper, was paid $90 a month and teachers at the West Side and East Side Schools were paid $40-50 a month. Porter's daughter Margaret married Harlan Curd in 1908. Their daughter, Mary Ellen Curd Simon (Mrs. E. J.), lives in Carbondale.

112 South Poplar, home of E. K. Porter. The lawn on the north extended to West Main Street. Currently the Walker Funeral Home, the house has been changed extensively.

605 West Walnut. This house was built in 1901 for George Washington Smith, a history professor at SINU, and father of Clyde L. Smith. This picture was taken in 1909. Maycock describes the house as "one of the finest examples of transitional Queen Anne/Colonial Revivial architecture remaining in Carbondale."

405 West Walnut. This house, built in 1899 for Andrew Caldwell, was torn down in 1956 when St. Francis Xavier Catholic Church was built. Photo was taken in 1907.

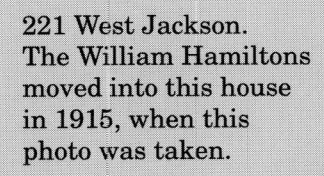

221 West Jackson. The William Hamiltons moved into this house in 1915, when this photo was taken.

39

500 Block of South Illinois. Built by Henry Sanders, this house occupied six acres between Illinois and Normal Avenues. Judge William J. Allen lived in it from 1875 until 1887, after which Dr. John Salter lived there. In 1891 it became the Keeley Institute, for treating drug and alcohol addiction. In the late 1890s it became the home of Will Hewitts, and then of Dr. John S. Lewis, Sr. This photo, taken in 1910, is the Lewis family. The information on the back reads, "Grandfather and Grandmother (Agnes Rush Lewis) on bench at left / Orman Lewis, Dr. Roscoe Lewis and Mother standing by horse with John Shelby Lewis, Jr., on horse / Great-Grand Father Lewis (Geo. Lewis) and Aunt Fern at right." In 1912 Dr. John S. Lewis, Sr., established the Amy Lewis Hospital in this house; Dr. J. W. Barrow and Dr. Roscoe Lewis were associates. The latter, who then owned the building and grounds, gave it to the Methodists. In 1916 it was expanded and named Holden Hospital. After being further built onto in 1922 and 1943, it was closed in the 1960s and demolished in 1976.

41

# JOHNSON, VANCIL, TAYLOR COMPANY

The basement housed the "bargain" area, mostly filled with household items.

Southwest corner of Jackson and North Illinois Avenue. The Johnson, Vancil, Taylor Company opened in 1917 and later moved to South Illinois Avenue, when it was called simply Johnson's. Later Archie Stroup bought it, renaming it Stroup's, and then Lita and Frank Bleyer bought it from Stroup and renamed it Bleyers.'

Men's Furnishings and Shoe Department, main floor of the Johnson, Vancil, and Taylor store. Note the basket used to send material across the store. The dry goods department was also on the main floor.

Ladies and Children's Ready-to-Wear Department was on the second floor.

Interior of the William H. Barrett Cash Store, located in the north half of a building at 1216 South Thompson Street (approximately where the Student Center stands on the SIU campus). Mr. Barrett and his wife Rosie moved to Carbondale from Mulkeytown in 1924 with their five children. They lived at 1218 South Thompson, where Mrs. Barrett operated a boarding house for male students. The Barretts also operated a restaurant and a gasoline station. Later, W.W. Trobaugh ran a Texaco station there and Mr. and Mrs. Howard (parents of Mrs. Victor Randolph) operated the restaurant. In 1948 the university bought the property and used it as the Agriculture Building.

Left: Street scene of the October 31, 1914, Halloween Parade. By 1926 the event had grown to a major celebration called "the great annual Fall Halloween Festival;" plans for that year were for "the most impressive ever witnessed in this city," according to tthe *Herald*. The committee consisted of Fred Held, chair, Charles Easterly, Nyle Huffman, John Y. Stotlar, and E. G. Lentz. Chairmen were named for finance, exposition, publicity, illumination, floats, trucks, music, parade, prizes and judges, concessions, policy and parking. The exposition was held under a tent between the depot and Illinois Avenue. A style show was a new feature to be added that year. By 1931, a *Herald* headline noted: "Hallowe'en Cost $2,181.73 for Last Year." The report of the treasurer Ira McLaughlin noted that the "two chief sources of revenue were the the big Hallowe'en dance and the sale of Hallowe'en buttons." The dance was held at the shoe factory (a building on North Illinois Avenue, financed by the Businessmen's Association to bring a shoe factory to Carbondale. When the shoe factory did not materialize, the New Era Dairy went into the building instead, at a later date). McLaughlin also noted that the balance from the previous event was $431.94 but that only $121.77 was on hand for the next year.

Above: Another annual event celebrated in Carbondale regularly was the Fourth of July. This picture, taken in 1907, shows one entry in the July 4 Parade. One of the children riding on the float in Francis "Hank" Renfro, whose father owned the bakery. Hank's son, Charles Renfro, is currently president of the First National Bank and Trust.

Below: A minstrel show in 1909. Frances Dillinger Reid writes that her Dad, "Connie" Dillinger, was in the group, as well as Mae Ward, Cecil Armstrong, Harry Rude, George Campbell, Roscoe Schutte, Sr., and some of the Pattersons. It was likely staged at the Old Opera House or in one of the churches.

Northwest Corner of East Main and Marion: Carbondale City Hall.

Previously the city had rented the third floor of Chapman's building. Although the property on this corner had been bought by the city in 1906, the new building was not constructed until 1914. To finance it, the city gave a 99-year lease to the Masons, who paid $9,000 to lease the third floor. The National Guard company just being formed leased the second floor. The first floor housed the city offices, council, jail, and fire department. The city of Carbondale put $20,000 into the project. It was used as a city hall until 1977, when it burned.

1907, West Main Street, from Normal Avenue looking east to Illinois Avenue. The Schwartz Building, the large one on the corner in the foreground, was one of the first built to accommodate multi-family housing needs.

The Phillips Supply Company (owned by Otis B. Phillips) on East Main Street (east of the bank building on the corner) in 1911 purchased the largest order of farm combines (from the Acme Queen Company) for southern Illinois.

45

# WWI

World War I: Walker Schwartz and army buddies in Luxemberg, 1918.

In their uniforms are John I. Wright and Claude Wright, the former was mayor ___; the latter a Carbondale dentist.

The home front during World War I. Carbondale obviously was aware of the War, but the immediate effect on the community was not greatly registered.

Fourth of July parade. One obvious observance of the War is witnessed in this parade.

46

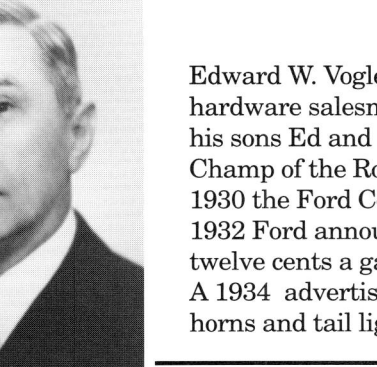

Edward W. Vogler, Sr. (1893-1970). Born in Belleville, Vogler travelled in southern Illinois as a hardware salesman after serving in World War I. In 1923 he bought the Ford agency. Later, his sons Ed and Don joined him in the business. In 1930 he was the Horseshoe Pitching Champ of the Rotary and Lions Clubs; he had served as Rotary President in 1929. In January 1930 the Ford Company announced that colors were added to the line of Model A Fords. In 1932 Ford announced the new Ford, with a V8 cylinder engine. Although gasoline had been twelve cents a gallon in 1929, in 1931 it went down to nine cents at the Martin Oil Company. A 1934 advertisement on Ford featured as standard equipment safety glass throughout, twin horns and tail lights, two sun visors, and cigar lighters. Vogler had owned part of the Murphysboro agency, but sold it in 1932, and the Metropolis agency, but sold it in 1934, although he kept the Pinckneyville agency. In 1935 he opened a branch at Carterville. An advertisement in 1935 featured the Ford with the V8 engine as the only car less than $2300. The first advertisement for the Lincoln was run in Carbondale in 1936, a V12, with 14 to 18 miles per gallon, for $1,275. Also, in 1936 a motor tune-up was available for $1.49.

301 North Illinois Avenue: Vogler Motor. A flour mill stood at this location in the late nineteenth century. In 1926 E. W. Vogler bought it, and in its place erected a $100,000 Ford agency, which celebrated its grand opening in 1928. The basement, recalls E. W. Vogler, Jr., was dug with a horse-drawn scoop. The structure, using an I-beam of steel, was built to last. Later, when the airfield north of Carbondale closed, Vogler bought the metal from the hangar and used it in an addition on the north end of the building. Photo ca 1930s.

500 Block of North Illinois Avenue. The C.I.P.S. ice plant provided cooling for innumerable Illinois Cenral refrigerator cars as well as innumerable lemonades and Kool-Aids for the people of Carbondale. Photo ca. 1920s.

47

300 Block West Jackson. During this period, this Jackson Street area (now all Memorial Hospital parking) was tree-lined with turn of the century homes, very popular because of their proximity to the heart of the town and the business district.

The Airport north of Carbondale. Going out to see the airplanes was a favorite activity in 1927. Pictured here are Midge Davis, Jane Warren, Rhoda Mae Baker, and Jean Smith.

The Chamber of Commerce in front of the Walnut Street Baptist Church in 1936. From the 1936 *Obelisk*: "The Chamber of Commerce proposes to create in commerce students an interest in commercial life and to furnish them with some social recreation. Meetings are devoted to a discussion of modern business problems and moving pictures of American industry." The fall term president was Robert Gallegly. This group is pictured after a homecoming breakfast.

An electric railway, known as "the trolley," ran from the Franklin Hotel in Carbondale to Murphysboro from about 1917 to 1927.

The Barth Theatre. Built in 1919 at a cost of over $32,000 this movie house on Monroe Street (200 block, across from the current GTE building) brought Hollywood entertainment to Carbondale. Prices in the early 20s were ten cents and fifteen cents for matinees, ten cents and twenty five cents for nights, but when sound movies arrived, the prices went up to twenty five and fifty cents. The first movie with sound to be shown in Carbondale was *Harmony at Home*. Sometimes the Barth held "pal nights" on Tuesday, when two could go for the price of one. The Barth name was changed to The Gem and then to The Rogers, which remained until the building burned. During the 1930s Carbondale vacillated on whether movies should be allowed on Sunday afternoon. In the photo to the right is the George Young laundry.

49

The Smith Family in 1924: from left to right: Frances Adams Smith and husband Russell Eugene Smith; Clyde L. Smith and wife Mary Smith; Nettie Caroline Adams Smith and husband George Washington Smith.

A 1933 Cub Scout Pack, photo taken at the home of Earl Goddard (312 West Main): from left to right: Pack Leader Harold Catt; Bill Townes (athlete and coach); Everett Earl Goddard (Dean, School of Business, Oregon State); Charles Marberry (Professor of Economics, University of Iowa); Howard Catt; Jim Marberry (teacher); and David Kenney (Professor Emeritus, Political Science, SIU).

Among the simple pleasures of childhood in Carbondale during this period was swinging in the backyard: Tom Barnes and Tom Schwartz, in the West College-Hays Street neighborhood.

Two Carbondale businessmen, ca. early 1940s: I. W. Dill and J. E. Etherton.

Another common pastime was sitting on the porch steps and celebrating children's birthday parties. Taken on June 12, 1926, at 609 West Walnut on David Kenney's birthday (he's in the center) were his sister Margaret (left) and a cousin, Margaret Harmon. Note the children's racecar on the porch.

Just fooling around in 1938 were Betty Berry and Susan Frier. Betty's family owned the neighborhood grocery on the corner of South Poplar and West College Street.

51

# Businesses

The Mobilgas station (with gravity pumps) at the corner of West Walnut and South Illinois, in the late 30s.

Across from the Mobil station, Fox's Drugstore was on the northwest corner of that intersection of Walnut and Illinois.

Across Walnut Street from Fox's was the Cox Hotel, operated by William and Violet Woodhouse Cox, who bought the frame, two-story building in the early 1930s, for $15,000, and operated a rooming house upstairs. Rooms were $1.50 to $2.00 per night. A restaurant was on the first floor. Next door, at 302 South Illinois, Violet operated a dry goods store, which some people told her would never attract business because it was too far down on South Illinois. The frame building burned in 1968 and was replaced by the current brick building. In the late 60s the Cox family had a Men's and Boys' Clothing store in the corner; behind that were a barber shop, a beauty shop, and a dry cleaners—all facing Walnut. The dry cleaners, Peerless, later moved across the alley.

South Illinois Avenue, looking north from the Walnut Street intersection. Ca. 1940, on the left were Fox's Drug Store, Johnson's Dry Goods, Maloney's shoe repair; on the right were the Mobilgas station, the Yellow Cab Company, and CIPS. Upstairs on both sides were offices of doctors, dentists, tailors, and seamstresses.

The Yellow Cab Company, at that time operated by Earl Throgmorton, but it was bought in 1939 by Philip Kimmel, who operated it until he died in 1980. In 1936 a Yellow Cab cost ten cents to any place in town.

The Bus Depot, 411-417 South Illinois, was built to accommodate the bus passenger traffic, which was taking over some of the railroad passenger traffic, especially since most of the railroad traffic toward the east had ceased to operate.

*The Herald* staff in 1942, from left to right: Tom Langdon, Editor B. J. Murrie of the Illinois Baptist, Mrs. Gilbert Pritchett, Fred Armstrong, Bert E. Hill, Gilbert Pritchett, Miss Mattie Lou Murrie, William B. Inman, Mrs. Mina Hilton, and Mrs. D. H. Cameron, Editor and Publisher. *The Herald,* established in 1892, was managed and edited by John Harris Barton from 1894 using the title *Southern Illinois Herald.*

The West Main Street side of the Hub corner (southwest corner of Main and Illinois) in 1939. Dr. John S. Lewis, Jr., who owned the building, had his office upstairs.

Below: The Good Luck Glove Company began operation in 1929. According to a May 2, 1929, article in *The Herald,* "C. T. Houghton and Company, manufacturers of jersey and canvas gloves, announce the opening of their factory Monday for instructions to forty-five girls who will then begin work Tuesday morning at the new factory. . . . the management expects to add additional help until some 150 workers will be on the payroll."

The Illinois National Guard Armory. Completed in 1937, this facility was one of the numerous WPA projects in Carbondale. It continues to serve the Guard.

The Illinois Department of Public Health Laboratory, at the corner of Chautauqua and South Oakland, was another WPA project, built ca 1940-41.

The home of John Y. and Constance Stotlar, at 705 West Main, pictured in 1920. The children are, left to right, Raymond Stotlar, Lewis Taylor, James Mitchell and Elizabeth Mitchell. Later this was the home John and Monte Stotlar.

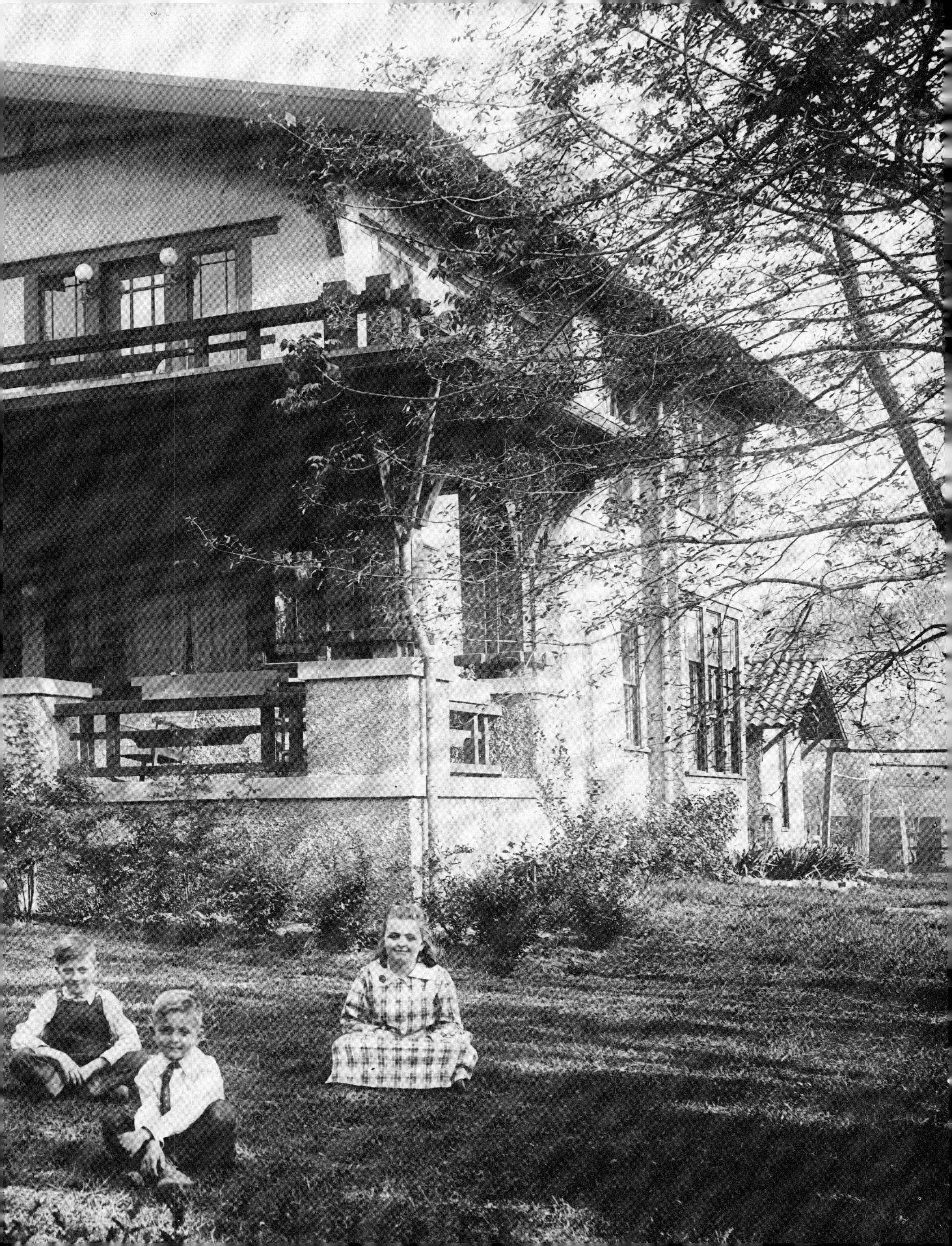

# Harry Lutz

On these two pages is a photographic history of one Carbondale native in this period, Harry Lutz (1907-1973), the son of Flaura and Henry Lutz, who lived in the first block of South Forest, off West Main Street.

In 1908, with parents Flaura and Henry Lutz, at 106 South Forest.

In 1907, in his carriage.

In 1910 on his tricycle.

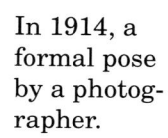

In 1914, a formal pose by a photographer.

58

In 1925-26 as a senior at Carbondale Community High School. The *Dial* notes, in basketball, "Dutch," a star of three years was chosen to pilot the team throughout the season which he did in a very praiseworthy manner. "They don't make 'em too fast for this good lookin' sheik to guard and as a natural result he made the all-star team at the tournament." He also played on the football team, on which the *Dial* reports, "Reason no one but Carbondale defeated Murphysboro for the first time in the annals of History. Harry put over the touchdown that enabled Carbondale to win, thus making a hero of himself and the rest of the team. . . . played a good game both defensive and offensive."

Harry Lutz married Betty Berry.

As a college student at SINU, Harry continued to play (for four years) both basketball and football. The 1930 *Obelisk* states, "Harry Lutz, a senior and four year man on the S.I.N.U. football team, was the backfield leader. Lutz was one of the best ball carriers on the team and a player who always gave all he had for the success of the team."

Above: the Lutz family at a Christmas, 1947, reunion.

Betty Berry Lutz, daughter Elizabeth, Harry Lutz in 1966. Lutz was a teacher and coach in Centralia, Illinois.

59

# Ridgway's Store

J. H. Ridgway moved to Carbondale after the turn of the century and located a small grocery business at 208 South Illinois Avenue. This picture, taken in 1912, shows Mr. Bass, on the far left, and Mabel Lipe, J. H. Ridgway, Earnest Searcy, Ralph Brandon, Oliver Briggs, and Mr. Wilhelm.

Ridgway's small grocery prospered and grew into a major business in Carbondale. He moved his operations to 115-117 North Washington, the interior of which is shown in this early 1930s photograph. Ridgway attributed his success to his credit service for customers.

A Drawing for Cash in 1941 at Ridgway's.

# WWII

## RETURN HOME

During World War II Carbondale men in the military service returned home when on leave. Many had their pictures taken and displayed at Entsminger's, on North Illinois Avenue, a favorite spot of the young people in Carbondale.

61

In 1931 the Businessmen's Association encouraged the Kroger company to locate division offices and a warehouse in Carbondale. The structure, on North Illinois Avenue, burned during World War II, and was rebuilt. When Kroger left Carbondale, Tuck Industries took over the building.

Frank Waldron operated Waldron' Store, just beyond the city limits on Route 13 East from 1941 to 1945. He sold the property to the state, to make room for the new highway.

The first block south of Main on Illinois Avenue, with traffic moving in both directions and metered parking spaces on both sides of the street, driving on Illinois Avenue was not easy.

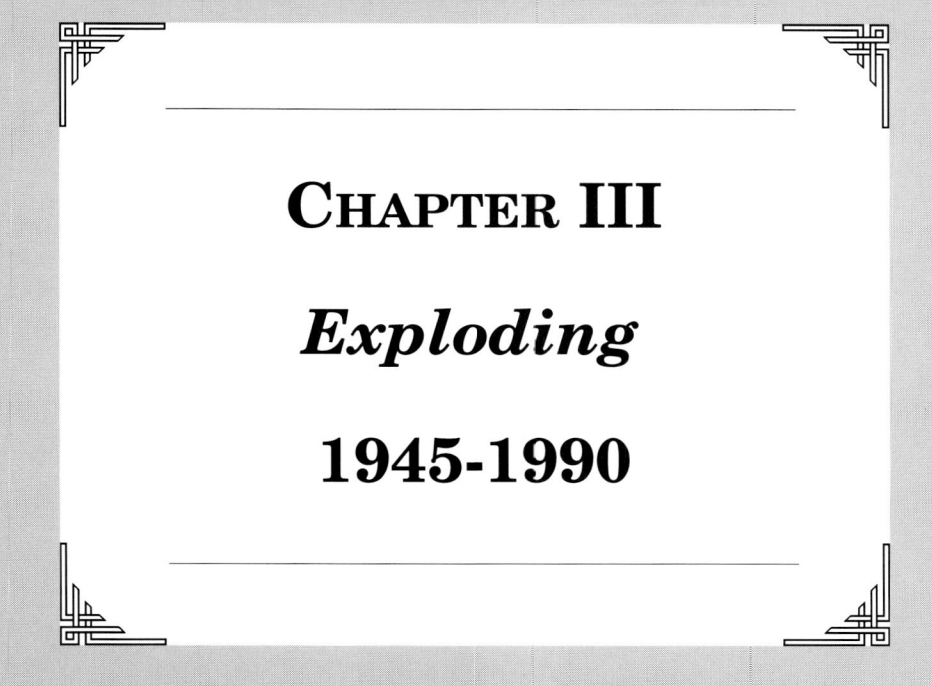

# Chapter III

## *Exploding*

## 1945-1990

The fall of 1945 was relatively quiet in Carbondale. Servicemen had not yet returned in any numbers from World War II, and the SIU campus was sparsely populated. In many ways Carbondale was like the other small towns in southern Illinois: rural, slow-paced, not very exciting. Between 1940 and 1950 the census grew by 2,361 to 10,911, probably accountable by the veterans who came with their families to the University in the late 40s. In the fall of 1945, SINU enrollment was 1,073 students, and by 1948 (after the change to University status in 1947 and after the return of many WW II veterans), the "post-war peak" was 3,013.

The local families returned to their routines, adding to their houses, starting small businesses, keeping up their social lives, and sharing in the activities of the University. Undoubtedly the major event was the arrival of Delyte W. Morris on September 10, 1948, to take the presidency of the University (though the townspeople at the time were totally unaware). From the time he arrived, Carbondale changed radically. (Details of his influence are included in the University chapter.) The immediate impact, however, lay in his realization that the campus had to expand, to accommodate the increasing enrollments. That expansion had a far-reaching effect on the community. Within the first three months of his being here, he met with Senator Crisenberry about the possibility of rerouting U.S. 51 south of town. At his inauguration on May 5, 1949, he spelled out his plan for the growth of the University, and on his numerous visits with all varieties of civic groups in Carbondale and the area, his intention became more and more obvious. The University would expand to include the south side of Mill Street (from Illinois to Oakland); the east side of Oakland (from Mill to Chautauqua); both sides of Chautauqua (excluding the State Lab) from Oakland to Thompson; Thompson from Grand to the outskirts of town; both sides of Grand from Oakland to Illinois: all an integral part of Carbondale at that time, with residences on almost every lot. In fact, Morris moved into the house next door to the Baptist Foundation (southwest corner of Grand and Thompson), and soon after he took over the Bradley house, to the south, for an office.

Maycock summed up this period, "The effects of this expansion on Carbondale were wide-spread and long-lasting, irreversibly altering the character and cohesion of the city. Changes were sometimes made hastily to meet immediate needs, but they often set patterns that continued, and the city is still [ca. 1980] grappling with many problems stemming from this period. These changes and their legacy of current problems generally fall into three areas: changes caused by the actual physical expansion of the university; new construction and demolition or conversion of older buildings to meet housing shortages; and new traffic patterns and commercial pressures caused by vast outward expansion of the city." "The most immediate effects were the result of the actual physical growth of the university, encroaching on residential neighborhoods, altering streets, and necessitating the demolition of numerous houses. While the first postwar building (Pulliam Hall, 1949) did not actually displace any houses, its location north and west of the original campus set a trend toward outward expansion into the town. [Note: This location had been decided prior to Morris' arrival.] Soon residential neighborhoods and streets ringing the university were directly affected, as houses were gradually taken over for university office space or demolished to make room for new buildings or parking lots."

From 1950 to 1960, the census went up by almost 4,000 to 14,671, but the University enrollment jumped from 3,087 in 1950 to 9,028 in 1960. With students included, the population of Carbondale almost doubled in the 50s, a decade that brought an explosion of development and problems. In the mid-50s, two primary factors led to a lessening of both freight and passenger railroad traffic: the decrease in the amount of coal being shipped, including that used by the railroad itself—with the advent of the diesel engine, and the completion of the U.S. Interstate Highway program and increase of private automobiles for distance travel. Thompson Lake, the retreat of many Carbondale citizens, was eliminated when the University bought the entire area and built dormitories on both sides. Subdivisions mushroomed in all directions, but mostly to the west. To meet the housing need for married students, the University also built family housing in the area east of the railroad, between Grand and Pleasant Hill Road (Southern Hills), influencing the development of the area east of Wall Street. Parking had become a major problem, and traffic patterns were impossible. By 1957 the Board of Trustees of SIU had banned cars for freshmen. But the worse was yet to come.

Boom and construction, as well as destruction later, marked the 1960s. From 1960 to 1970 the Carbondale census rose by 55% to 22,816, while in the same period SIU enrollment increased by 150%, from 9,028 to 22,625. Over 17,000 additional people came to Carbondale between 1960 and 1970, and the town, not prepared, reeled under the problems: water, sewer, schools, traffic, as well as cultural, economic, and social. SIU expanded to more areas east of the railroad to University Park, and Morris developed a new Master Plan for the campus. The decade had begun on an up-swing, with much construction both on campus and in town. But as Maycock reports, "Rapid increases in the number of faculty and students after the war, but particularly in the 1960s, created unprecedented demands for housing in Carbondale. Houses were demolished to construct apartment buildings, and enterprising landlords bought up large single-family houses and converted them to rental units. The houses most easily adapted were large late nineteenth-century Queen Anne houses such as 309 West Main (1895) and 501 West Walnut Street, which became apartments or boardinghouses. Some earlier nineteenth-century houses such as 416 West Main Street (1868) were also vulnerable and were remodeled into numerous apartments and allowed to deteriorate until they were considered eyesores and there was pressure for demolition. The effect on the city's nineteenth-century architecture and neighborhoods was particularly severe. Most of the converted houses were located in older residential areas, near downtown and within walking distance of the university. Density in these neighborhoods increased, and maintenance often declined, making them less desirable to live in. Houses were increasingly in the hands of absentee landlords, population became more transient, and owner occupants began to move away from these older areas into new subdivisions of single-family houses being laid out east and west of the old city limits. The subdivisions west of

Oakland Avenue seemed particularly attractive to university professors and other professionals, and their success encouraged development even further west."

Long-time residents recall an element of people, commonly known as hippies and not thought to be students necessarily, who created a variety of disturbances. They were characterized by their dirty, disheveled appearance, their ragged clothing or lack of it, their general disorderliness and revolt. Though in the early part of the decade they were placid and leaned toward folk music and liberal attitudes, toward the end they turned to chaos. On the campus, the Agriculture Building was bombed in 1968, Old Main was burned in 1969, and in May, 1970, an element rioted, trashed Illinois Avenue, and the University closed. There was an air of militancy as Carbondale had a curfew and the National Guard.

In the 1970s, though the census rose from 22,816 to 26,414, there seemed to be a levelling off. In 1972 Carbondale was named All American City. The Vietnamese War ended in 1974. The students changed, and the townspeople seemed to breathe a sigh of relief and attempted to resume some kind of normalcy. As Maycock summarized, ". . . by the late 1970s the steady progression west had crossed Tower Road. Some expansion also took place on the east and beyond the southern boundary of the city with the development of Heritage Hills, but the most significant push was definitely to the west toward Murphysboro. This shift in population away from the central city has created new traffic patterns and greater traffic problems than the currently [1980] twenty-six-thousand population figures would indicate. As new residential areas have developed in the far east and west, the city as a comprehensible walking space has become a thing of the past, and the effect on Carbondale's early architecture has been severe. Those who live in the older residential neighborhoods east of Oakland and west of Wall Street can still walk or bicycle to both downtown and the university. Much of the population, however, now lives beyond these limits and relies primarily on the automobile for transportation. This has caused the development of extensive strip shopping areas east and west along Illinois Route 13 and a regional shopping mall east of the city, all of which are designed to be accessible primarily by car. Even the post office moved in the 1970s from its central location on Main Street to a site along a divided highway east of the city. . . . As business has become more automobile-oriented and moved to the eastern and western fringes of the city, Carbondale's downtown has declined in both function and appearance. No longer the commercial hub of the city, the public square has lost its identity and nineteenth-century importance. Many long-established businesses have moved from the square to the new outlying shopping areas, and many of the early buildings have been demolished."

The population increased hardly at all from 1980 to 1990. The community seems to have settled into a peaceful co-existence with the University, with commercialism (in spite of efforts to bring in industry) primarily centering around the medical profession and the retail trade. In fact, most of the growth of the 1980s was in these two areas. The University had a slight decline in the mid 1980s, dropping in enrollment and support staff from 1984 to 1987, when there began an incline in figures. Certainly Carbondale in the last two decades has become an unusual place in southern Illinois, most unlike the other communities surrounding it. The air is frequently an international one, a cosmopolitan atmosphere punctuated by many cultures, dress, and tongues. The pace is fast, both in traffic and in life itself. Carbondale is inundated with fast food restaurants, but unfortunately not with other, more conventional ones. Markets and stores cater to the college students and to those who are not native to the United States. But many opportunities abound: lectures, concerts, sports events, theaters, and bars constantly beckon to the population. Living in Carbondale is interesting, exciting, and ever-changing.

In 1951 this typical scene at the corner of Main and Illinois represents a traffic officer's nightmare. However, Carbondale had no traffic officers at that time.

# SIU Housing

By the mid-fifties the SIU enrollment was doubling, and housing was scarce because private developers had not yet moved into Carbondale to provide new dormitories. The Greek organizations were also growing and seeking adequate houses for their groups. For the most part they turned to the large, old homes, close to the campus and probably originally built for faculty members. Representative here are such groups and the houses they occupied.

715 South Washington was home for Sigma Tau Gamma. The house, which has since been demolished, was large and rambling and barely adequate.

608 West College housed the Delta Chi fraternity for a number of years. Emil Spees, who lived there as an undergraduate, recalls the house well: it had a number of bedrooms (but very small closets), a kitchen, living room, dining room, and another big room at the back that served as a study room. Although no requirement for a resident adult existed, the number of veterans in the group dictated that noise was kept to a decent level—it was a residential neighborhood—and that a good rapport with the neighbors was sought.

The Delta Zetas rented this house at 320 West Walnut, a bit farther from the campus.

Kappa Alpha Psi fraternity lived at 719 S. Washington, which according to the '56 *Obelisk* was newly decorated inside and out. Twenty men lived here.

700 South University was the Theta Xi house, which they noted was close to UDs.

800 South University was probably the only house built to accommodate group living. Mr. Stotlar built it for the Delta Sigma Epsilon (which later became Alpha Gamma Delta) chapter. Unlike the men's groups, there was a housemother who made certain that the girls kept study hours and house rules. In those days women had to be in their houses by 10:30 on weekday nights, but they could stay out until midnight on Saturday night. Breaking the rules resulted in being campussed.

# TRAFFIC

The 700 block of South Illinois Avenue in the 60s reveals the kind of traffic that Carbondale faced.

A typical traffic jam when too many students had cars, and the early morning rush to classes was bedlam.

The corner of Harwood and Thompson, where now the Faner sidewalk carries strictly pedestrian traffic, this corner was on South 51 before it was rerouted on the east side of the gymnasium (now Davies Gym), where tennis courts had been.

In 1948 when Mr. Truman was a candidate for the presidency, he visited Carbondale. With him in the car are Senators Douglas and Dirksen.

Some years later in 1960 John F. Kennedy was on the same campaign trail. Helping him with a hand up is Bill Etherton, and looking after in the background is SIU security, Tom Leffler.

Ten years later, Carbondale's David Kenney signs "the document" at the Sixth Illinois Constitutional Convention.

Hamilton's service station, at the corner of Oak and North Illinois in 1947, was typical of the time.

The Franklin Hotel as it appeared in the 1960s, when weekly and monthly tenants made the clientele. It originated in about 1858 as the Union House, at 200 North Illinois Avenue, and then was renamed the Planters House Hotel. It was the only brick hotel at the time. It was demolished in 1991.

The high-rise dormitories, Brush Towers, built in the 60s on the east side of the railroad tracks appear on the horizon from all approaches to Carbondale.

Before the stands on the east side of the stadium were added, the view was pastoral; now over the top the Brush Towers are the only sight.

In 1952 the First National Bank at 101 North Washington held open house after an extensive remodelling. Paying a visit are the Ethertons: J. E. Etherton, his son, Bill Etherton, Julia Mitchell Etherton (wife of J. E.), and Helen Etherton (wife of Bill).

71

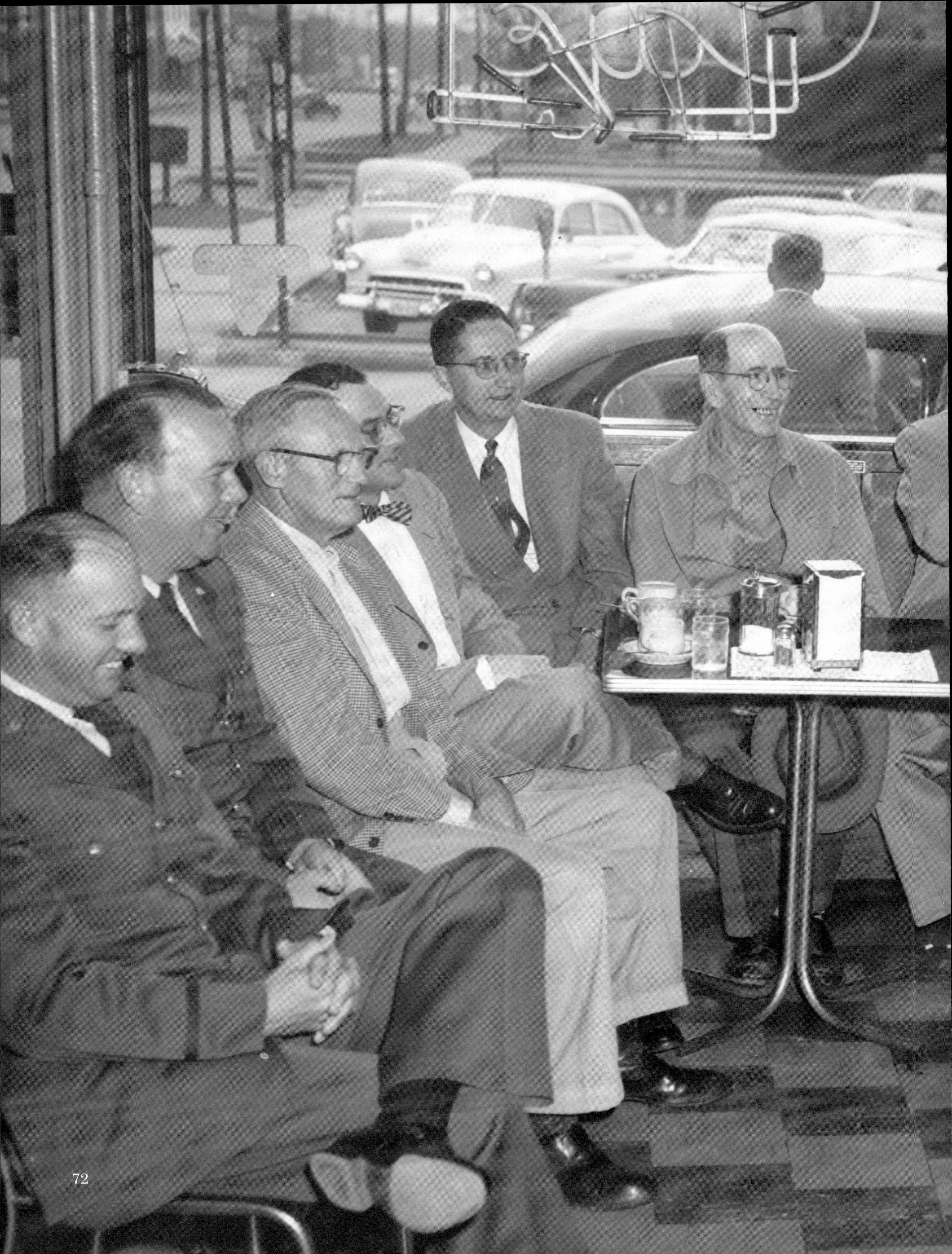

Morning coffee at the Hub was a ritual. Seated left to right, Benny Vicory (SIU ROTC),—Timm (also ROTC), General Robert Davis, Everett Prosser, John G. Gilbert, John "Jock" Williams, B. Haddon Davenport, Dr. "Spider" Wright, Harry Goetz, I. W. Dill, Walker Schwartz, J. E. "Ebb" Etherton, and H. A. "Nick" Masters, proprietor of the Hub. ca. 1950s.

The Ritz Cafe, taken in the 1940s, was one of the few that stayed open all night.

Established at 508 South Illinois Avenue, the Dairy Queen has become a landmark, serving both the townspeople and the students, who drive and walk there, and frequently sit on the curb of Illinois Avenue to enjoy their treats.

The City Dairy, built in 1941 at 521 South Illinois Avenue, was a curved brick building (like that used on the Varsity Drug corner). The basement, according to James Morris who owned the building, was dug by Mr. Cecil, who used mules and a scraper. The brick work was done by Dewey Potts.

The Varsity Drug Store (when it was really a drug store) in the 1930s.

The Varsity corner, rounded with art deco trim, also taken in the 1930s.

The Varsity Theater, for many years (after the Rogers burned), was the only movie theater in Carbondale. Ca. 1930s.

75

The WCIL Breakfast Club at the Roberts Hotel in 1948. Seated, left to right, Ada Rowan, Wilda Rudmose, Anne E. Searing, Paul H. McRoy, Ann McRoy, Ida Garman, Dave Garman, and Paul McRoy (owner, WCIL); standing, waiter, Alma Hankla, MC Ralph Wayne.

University Drugs and Cafeteria, 819 South Illinois, built in 1947 by Martin Chaney, was the closest commercial venture to the campus, excluding Carter's Cafe on the corner of Grand and University Avenues.

An interior view of UD's, as it was called —the soda fountain.

76

Another landmark in Carbondale, Dillinger's Store at 109 South Washington.

In the store, J. C. Dillinger, who willingly gives advice on all kinds of gardening and farming problems as well as selling the products that go with.

Jim and Ruth's Market, West Hickory, represents one of the very few remaining independent grocers in Carbondale.

Jim Temple, who bought the store in the 1950s, cuts meat in the midst of his museum-like setting.

77

Above: IDOT (Illinois Department of Transportation), better known to the locals as the highway office, came to Carbondale in 1919, and was located in the Brush Building, over the Hub Cafe. In 1925 the office moved to the third floor of the First National Bank Building, and in June 1941, it moved for the last time to its present location on old route 13 west. The first building, 8350 square feet of offices plus garage and sign shop, cost $168,000. In 1956 it was expanded with an additional 5,000 square feet of office and 10,000 square feet of storage and heating plant, costing $404,000. In 1961 it was remodeled, and in 1965 additional Materials Lab and Maintenance storage was added. The Local Roads Annex was added in 1986, the west wing in 1988, and extensive remodeling followed. Photo ca. 1982.

W. Troy Barrett and his son Tom, at 518 South Illinois. Troy (in 1991 the oldest full-time practicising attorney in Jackson County) and his family lived in the rear of the house, with his offices in the front, from 1955 to 1966. At that time the area was primarily residential, although in the background is the City Diary building, which housed the Prosperity Cleaners at that time (1955).

The University Mall, new 13 east, opened in its first stage in 1974. Since then, it has been added to extensively.

78

Amateur dramatics have been part of life in Carbondale, from the early days to the present time. This production was in 1903 in the Moody Opera House (upstairs in the building at 101 North Washington). The building is currently occupied by the Stage Company. In this photo are, front row, left to right: John Bellamy, Raymond Parkinson, Clarence Joyner; second row: Lillian Gubleman, John Stotlar, Winifred Ellis, Harry Wilson, Donald Kirk; third row: Lillian Tanner, John Mimick, John Allen, Arthur Lee, Bessie Brush, John Doty, Roscoe Taylor; fourth row: Robert Teeter, B. F. Norfleet, Clyde Smith.

*Churches, schools, medical and banking facilities, the public library, recreation facilities, and social life are treated as units rather than as segments of the chronological overview.*

# CHAPTER IV

# *Public*

# *Institutions*

# CHURCHES

Daniel H. Brush wrote in his memoirs, "I further propose that lots 59, 74, 99, and 114 should be reserved for donation to such churches as should first select and build thereon, which was assented to by all the proprietors present and entered upon the plat in the following words: 'The lots donated to churches as marked on this plat are not to vest in said churches until a house of worship shall be erected thereon of stone, brick, or frame, worth at least five hundred dollars, and then to vest in fee simple in such church.'" He also wrote, "The first sermon in the town was preached by Rev. Josiah Wood, a Presbyterian minister, in December, 1852. He preached in an unfinished log cabin erected by Asgill Conner for a dwelling, but having only the roof on and the floor laid."

The first church to select a lot, the Presbyterian, took lot 59 in February 1853, when the church was organized by Reverend Josiah Wood. Following that, the second, #99, was selected in 1856 by the Methodists, who had been organized in 1853 under Bishop Levi Scott, who appointed the Rev. T. C. Lopas as the first minister. The third, #74, went in 1868 to the Baptists, who had been organized in 1861 by William Lamer, Jonathan Wiseman, Thompson Williams, and Julia Williams. In 1868 the fourth lot, #114, went to the Christian Church, whose initiator and principle founder was Dr. Isaac Mulkey in 1862.

A typical adult study class, in 1921. Dr. Delia Caldwell was the teacher.

Taken about 1907, this Sunday School Class was taught by Mrs. Winchester.

# FIRST PRESBYTERIAN CHURCH

The Presbyterian church's first book of trustees record shows: "January 4, 1853—'This day, the Reverend Josiah Wood, a minister of the Presbyterian Church, acting for and one [sic] behalf of that church, selected Lot. No. 59, in said town for the purpose of erecting thereon, a house of worship. On the same date, a subscription paper was drawn up and some money subscribed to be paid to Asgill Conner and William Richart to be held by them until properly elected trustees should qualify to hold said property and proceed with the erection of a church thereon'." On February 13, 1854, Reverend Josiah Wood organized the church with the assistance of Rev. Robert Stewart of Greenville, Illinois. Members were Frances E. and Rowland R. Brush, Dr. William and Elizabeth Richart, and Mrs. Almira Doughty. Rowland R. Brush was elected elder. The church built on West Monroe Street (begun in 1856 and completed in 1859) cost $3,642.50. In 1869 the building was improved, at a cost of $400, to put it on stone pillars and to repair the inside: woodwork was refinished, book racks were put on the backs of the pews, blinds were added, "new chandeliers of four burners with lamps for kerosene oil were hung," the choir was moved from the back to the front and put on a new carpeted platform, the pew gates were removed, and the pulpit was placed in a lower, central position.

Around 1900 the Presbyterian Church established a mission at 310 E. Birch. It was supervised by Miss Amanda Templeton until she died in 1925, when it was abandoned.

In 1902 the congregation bought lots No. 185 and 186 of the Singleton Subdivision (on the northwest corner of Elm and Normal), at a cost of $1800. Isaac Rapp designed the new building, based on a church he had seen in Scotland. Stone was donated by Hugh Lauder and dressed at the Boskeydell quarry by J. J. Arnold. The new building, which cost $32,287.64, was dedicated in July 1907. In 1954 an extensive education wing was added, reusing the original stone on the exterior to give a unified appearance.

The First Presbyterian Church on Monroe Street (where the GTE building now stands). This building served the congregation from 1859 till 1907.

The Presbyterian Mission Chapel, at 310 East Birch, was established at about the turn of the century. Miss Amanda Templeton supervised it until 1925, when she died. Miss Templeton, an aunt of Mrs. W. L. Kenney, had been a missionary in the Southwestern United States, primarily among the Seminole Indians.

The First Presbyterian Church, corner of South University and West Elm, was dedicated in July 1907. The education wing to the right was added in 1954.

81

## FIRST BAPTIST CHURCH

The First Baptist Church was organized in 1861 by Elder A. Lisle at the Crowell School, southwest of Carbondale. Services were held in this school and at the Glade School House for a year, and then for several years in the Campbell grain house. The first building was built in 1869-71 on West North Street (now West Jackson) and served for thirty years. The cornerstone of the present building (corner of Main and University) was laid on October 12, 1902. Stone for the building came by railroad flats and horse team and wagon from Boskeydell. From May Dorsey's "Through the Years 1861-1980, First Baptist Church, Carbondale, Illinois," the October 15, 1902, *Free Press* had the following: "The corner stone to the new Baptist church was laid with appropriate ceremony Sunday afternoon. The designer of the building is S. A. Bullard of Springfield. The building will be 84 x 56' of cut sand stone and brick. It will have steam heat and be very modern. Cost about $15,000.00" The Baptists bought the Frank Chapman house, 304 West Main (built in 1868-69) as an annex in 1901. It was demolished in 1966 to allow for a new educational annex which was dedicated on October 15, 1967. The church belongs to the American Baptist Convention.

The original building of the First Baptist Church, in the 200 block of West Jackson Street. The building was begun in 1868 but not finished until 1871. The congregation met here until a new building was constructed in 1903. The building was demolished in 1977.

From 1901 the First Baptist Church used the Frank Chapman house, at 304 West Main (built in 1868-69 by Isaac Rapp), as an annex until it was demolished in 1966.

The lavishness of the interior of the Chapman house is shown by the ornate plaster work.

82

## WALNUT STREET BAPTIST CHURCH

The Walnut Street Baptist Church was organized in 1922; the congregation, who bought the northeast corner lot on Walnut and Normal, built in 1923 the present building, which has since been remodeled. The church is in the Southern Baptist Convention.

## UNIVERSITY BAPTIST CHURCH

In 1949 the University Baptist Church was organized; the congregation built the present facility on the southwest corner of Freeman and Oakland in two phases, the first in 1950, the second in 1958. This church is also in the Southern Baptist Convention.

The First Baptist Church, corner of Main and University, with the educational wing which was added in 1967.

The Walnut Street Baptist Church, corner of West Walnut and South University, built originally in 1923 and added onto in 1951.

University Baptist Church, built in two stages — 1950 and 1958, at the corner of South Oakland and West Freeman.

83

## FIRST METHODIST CHURCH

The Methodist congregation built "the Blue Church" in 1858 at 209 East Jackson Street at a cost of $1,000; it was 30 x 60 feet, with a small room added in the mid 1870s. It had two entrances and two "cannon ball" stoves to provide heat. According to the church's "Centennial Year 1853-1953" brochure, "Undoubtedly there was some kind of bell to call early worshippers to church services. At first a bell was mounted outside the building, but persons who recall the building say that a belfry was added later to house a bell. Since about 1867 the present bell in the tall spire of First Methodist Church has been calling its people to the house of worship. An unusual story relates to the acquisition of that bell, a circumstance arising out of the intense political zeal in the community following the end of the Civil War. The bell was a gift to the church from the proceeds of a political wager between a Frank J. Chapman and Ephriam Snyder. Chapman won and divided the winnings, $500.00, between the Methodist and the Presbyterian churches in the community. The Methodists took a bell which bears the name of Chapman and the date 1867. The Presbyterians took paint for their building." The first building was used for thirty years. The second was placed on lots 67, 68, and 69, bought in 1881 (the present site on West Main Street). A frame building, completed in 1888, cost $10,000 and served for thirty-five years. The present building was built in 1921-22.

During the pastorate of Dr. George E. McCammon (1903-09) the church sponsored the formation of Grace Methodist Church, which built on Marion Street and later moved to North Tower Road. Their previous building burned in 1925, was replaced in 1926, and was bought in the late 80s by the Good Samaritan Ministries.

The first Methodist church was built in 1858 on East Jackson Street; the second, shown in this photograph, was built on the site of the present church in 1888 and served for thirty-five years.

The present Methodist Church, built in 1921-22. This photograph was taken some years ago, before the brick parsonage on the west side was torn down, in 1967.

## FIRST CHRISTIAN CHURCH

Eleven members of the Mulkey, Yost, Blair, and Gilbert families organized the Christian Church on September 4, 1862, at the Granary; the main founder was Dr. Isaac Mulkey. After taking the fourth lot set aside for churches (on East Monroe Street at Washington), the congregation had the cornerstone laid for the building in 1866, but did not complete it until 1874. From Aileen Neely's "Days of Our Years" is the following: "The church was one of the finest buildings in the city and was used for a variety of community events. One of these was the 1896 showing of the first motion picture in town. The event was well remembered by church member Clyde Smith, who as a boy of ten, had been hired by the traveling exhibition to work the behind-the-scenes sound effects for this silent film." In 1899 the church bought three lots on Monroe Street for $1100, from Julia M. Bridges, and in 1901 they began the present building, for which George F. Barber (of Knoxville, Tennessee) was the architect. The estimated cost was $10,000, but actual was twice that. The *Free Press* described the building as: "The three art glass memorial windows and the woodwork of highly polished hand pine were mentioned as adding to the beauty of the interior. It was also mentioned that the second story was arranged so that it could be used as living quarters for the pastor, if desired." In 1950 extensive reconstruction to the church cost $79,264.76. In 1964 an educational wing was added. When Brush School burned on December 12, 1976, students used this church for temporary classrooms for the balance of the school year.

The First Christian Church, built in 1902.

The Banner Sunday School Class of the First Christian Church in 1914.

## ST. FRANCIS XAVIER CHURCH

In 1900 the Catholic families built a small church on South Poplar street and used it until 1958, when it was replaced by the present building on the next block of Poplar, between Elm and Walnut.

St. Francis Xavier Church, built in 1900, at the southeast corner of West Elm and South Poplar Streets, served the congregation until 1958.

The present St. Francis Xavier Church, on South Poplar, between Walnut and Elm Streets.

## ST. ANDREW'S EPISCOPAL CHURCH

In 1882 the "Mission of St. Andrew's" was approved, but the first record of services was not until 1895. The first building at 301 West Elm was dedicated in 1904. In 1926 that building was sold to the Carbondale Public Library, and the cornerstone for a new building on West Mill was laid. In 1958 St. Andrew's was granted parish status, with Father W. John Harris as rector. A new church was built next door to the old one in 1979.

The second building of St. Andrew's Episcopal Church, at 404 West Mill.

86

## ROCK HILL BAPTIST CHURCH

After being organized near Makanda, the Rock Hill Missionary Baptist Church was reorganized in 1871 by Rev. R. Grayson, and was located on East Walnut Street. During the pastorage of Rev. W. M. Moody the church was moved to its present location at 219 East Monroe Street in 1924. Rev. Lenus Turley became the pastor in November 1955, and since then the congregation has accomplished much in the way of refurbishing the church. Turley Park, on the corner of West Main and Glenview, is named for Rev. Turley, who died in 1969. About him it was said, "Rev. Turley always liked to build. He loved the positive approach to problems. He glorified in encouraging people, in helping people, and in looking at the bright side of things."

The Rock Hill Baptist Church, built in 1924 at 219 East Monroe Street.

## OLIVET FREE WILL BAPTIST CHURCH

In 1866 two Free Will Baptist ministers from Michigan, J. S. Manning and A. H. Chase, stopped in Carbondale on their way to Cairo. With their help thirty-five people founded the first Negro Church of Carbondale. They also helped to establish a school for Negro children in an old blacksmith shop and were instrumental in founding the East Side School, which was moved to the Attucks location. In 1916 while Rev. A. C. Moore was pastor, the church was renamed Olivet Free Will Baptist and was dedicated that year. In 1941 the North Illinois Avenue church was sold to Vogler Motor Co., and the cornerstone for the building at 409 N. Marion was laid. For almost 33 years Rev. Alonzo A. Crim served as pastor of this church while at the same time teaching at Attucks School, where he was on the first faculty.

Olivet Free Will Baptist Church, at 409 North Marion, in 1941.

## BETHEL AFRICAN METHODIST EPISCOPAL CHURCH

Organized in 1864 by the Reverend Ransom Grief in the home of Spencer Williams, the Bethel African Methodist Episcopal Church occupied a building on North Marion Street, but was moved to West Oak Street, where it remained for three years, and then to the present location at 316 East Jackson. However, that building burned, and the congregation met at Attucks School while a new church was built. In 1983 the church celebrated its 115th anniversary.

Bethel African Methodist Episcopal Church 115th Anniversary artist rendering.

# SCHOOLS

To meet the needs of education in the early years, according to Wright, "At the outset two town outlots had been set aside for school purposes, number 39 for a west side school and 30 for one on the east side. It was not until October, 1855, however, that the Carbondale School District was set up under the Free School Law, the district including the whole of Carbondale Township, and not until April, 1856, that the west side public school . . . was opened. Edmund Newsome says that it was put up in a few weeks, and it appears to have been a very modest building indeed." Maycock notes that it measured 20 x 30 feet, had a steeply pitched roof and center cross gable, and cost $500, paid by donations. Wright added that "Before that time there was a private school conducted by Miss Eliza Ann Richart . . . in a building on lot 28." Temporary facilities were called into use, as the number of children grew, until in 1914 in a special election, two new buildings were approved: In 1915 the Attucks was built at 410 East Main (replacing the old East Side School which had had six small rooms and 250 students), and Brush at 401 West Main (replacing the old West Side School). Both Attucks and Brush have been demolished.

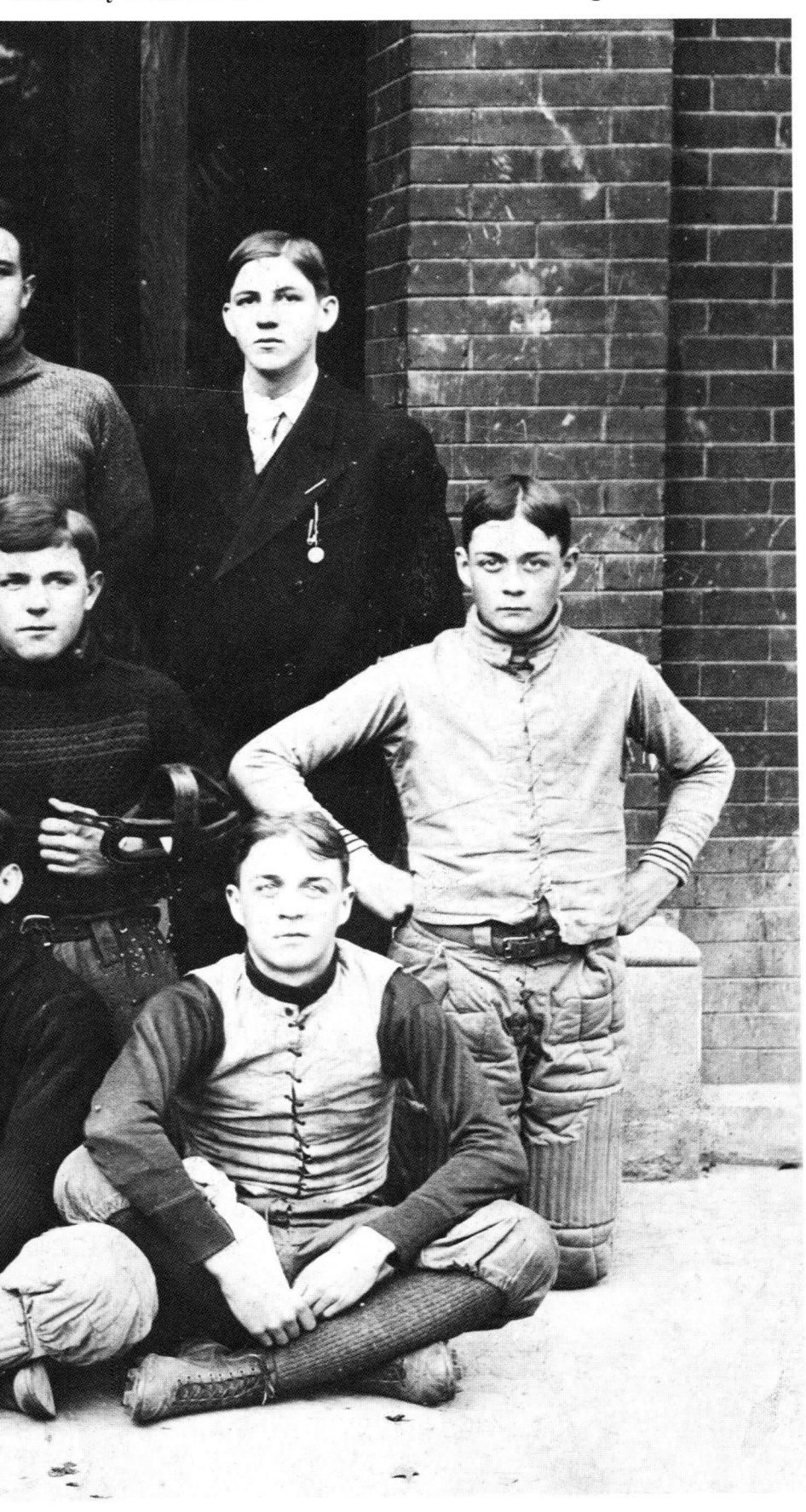

Carbondale College was established in 1856 by the Presbyterian Church at 501 South Washington. However, completion of the building met with complications. Carbondale citizens subscribed $1,045 to support the college, headed by James M. Campbell, who struggled with Daniel Brush to finish the building. But, according to Wright, "In 1863 the property was sold by the sheriff, and Campbell bid it in in order to save as much as possible for himself and Brush of their considerable investment. Something was salvaged finally when the Christian Church bought the property and changed its name to Southern Illinois College." After interim use during the war, the school opened in October 1866 under Rev. Clark Braden, who began with five pupils. He continued until 1870, when there were almost three hundred students, at all levels from elementary to college. It became a public school, with a name change to Lincoln, and served as the Carbondale High School

1906 football team. Known members are, left to right, first row: Harry House, Cy Louden, T. Penrod, Ben Fluck, Bill Baird, Ben Gillett; second row: Mel Rauch, ? , Claude Legg, Fred Comstock, Gilbert Entsminger; third row: ? , Elmer Christopher, Dolph Elmore, Dave Entsminger.

as well when in 1905 public education was extended to include grades nine through twelve. In 1906 a wing was added; in 1949 the building was razed, rebuilt, and the new building was added on to in 1957, 1965, and 1968.

In 1923 the new high school at 200 North Springer was completed and occupied. On September 16, 1936, a new gymnasium, built by the WPA, was dedicated. Additions to CCHS in 1949 were the present cafeteria, library, music room, and some classrooms; in 1960, science and foreign language classrooms, Bowen Gym, and across Oakland, the Frank Bleyer Football Field and the Reid Martin Athletic Field; and in 1967, the William McBride Learning Center. Also in 1967 an additional facility at 1301 East Walnut was completed.

The elementary district in 1924 put an addition on Brush School. In 1949 Springmore School was built on the corner of Springer and Sycamore (in 1974 the district gave the facility to the Carbondale Senior Citizens). Since Carbondale was experiencing growth in population in the 1950s and 1960s, more elementary schools were built: Winkler (at 1218 West Freeman), Lakeland (925 South Giant City Road), and Thomas (1205 North Wall) were built in 1955. At that time, Winkler was on the western edge of Carbondale. Glendale (1900 North Illinois) followed in 1958, Parrish (121 North Parrish Lane) in 1965, and Lewis (801 South Lewis Lane) in 1966.

Above: West Side School, built in 1856, served Carbondale school children on the west side of the railway until 1914, when Brush School was built to replace it.

Right: Brush School, 401 West Main, was used until it burned on December 12, 1976. It was demolished in 1980.

The seventh grade Brush School basketball team in 1937. Left to right, Bob Lynn, John "Bud" Stotlar, Bill Dyer, "Peanut" Jennings, Eugene Kettring, Carl Craine, and Paul _____. The teachers/coaches are not identified.

A class in 1914, at West Side School.

Attucks School. Photo Courtesy *Southern Illinoian*

The Lincoln Junior High School basketball team in 1922.

The old Carbondale College building, 501 South Washington, was renamed Lincoln School in 1905. These unidentified students and teachers sat for the photographer soon afterward.

The 1925 CCHS Homecoming Queen and Pages: Florence Newman, Gladys Holmes (queen), and Jane Federer.

The CCHS entrance, taken in 1930.

CCHS as it looked originally, in 1923, on North Springer Street.

93

1937 CCHS football team: undefeated, untied, unscored against all year, coached by Frank Bridges. Left to right, first row: Neal, Frey, Hunsaker, Keller, Lutz, Cox, Crawshaw, Harrell, Allen, Ellis, Gill. Back row: Bowen, Smith, Deason, McGinnis, Gilmore, Marberry, Allen, Wise, Chandler, Curtis, Kuehn, Townes, Coach Bridges. Needless to say, this team is still having reunions.

Above: CCHS after addition of gym on Springer Street. Photo taken 1949.

Below: CCHS, west side, with additions. In foreground is Bowen Gym.

Above: CCHS 1967 basketball team, which won second in the state tournament. Back row, left to right: Doug Woolard, Bob Crane, Brad Woods, David Walls, Terry Wallace, L. C. Brasfield, Peaches Lascer, Bill Perkins, Chuck Taylor, Phil Gilbert, Jesse Crowe, Kenny Lewis, Geoff Partlow, Gary Baggett; front row: Asst. Coach Walt Moore, Head Coach John Cherry, Doug Cherry, Asst. Coach Harold Emme.

Mrs. Fox's Brush School Class 1939-40.

95

Thomas School, built in 1955 at 1205 North Wall.

Lincoln Junior High School, 1949.

Parrish School, built in 1965 at 121 North Parrish Lane.

Springmore School, built in 1949 on the corner of Springer and Sycamore, now the Senior Citizens Center.

# BANKING IN CARBONDALE

Banking in the 1880s was apparently a sideline of some of the general merchants. James Moody Richart and Henry F. Campbell, Samuel E. North, Thomas E. North, John G. Campbell, and William Wykes operated retail stores, with some banking operations included. By 1885 William Wykes operated the City Bank of Carbondale; in 1870 H. B. Schuler began banking operations on the northwest corner of Main and Illinois, but the building burned and they moved across the square. During the Panic of 1893 both the Wykes bank and that of Richart and Campbell failed, and their three-story building on the northeast corner of Main and Washington sold.

The First National Bank and Trust (as it is known today) initially was organized, according to John W. D. Wright, as "a blessing in disguise, because they [the bank failures resulting from the Panic of 1893 and the depression that followed] led to the establishment of Carbondale's first sound, and important, banking institution, the First National Bank of Carbondale." This bank was chartered on May 25, 1893, in the state of Illinois, with $50,000 capital. The first president was Frank A. Prickett, the first vice president was William A. (Gus) Schwartz, and other board members were Judge O. A. Harker, Frank Clements, E. E. Mitchell, J. D. Peters, and James A. Pease (from Chicago). Prickett remained president until he died in 1903, by which time the residents of Carbondale had demonstrated confidence in the new bank. The bank was housed in the Richart and Campbell Building, which was remodelled in 1894 to include a store, the bank, and on the upper floors an enlarged opera house with seating for five hundred. The remodelling, directed by the architect Isaac Rapp, altered the exterior appearance of the building by changing some windows to circular ones, adding a dormer, a new roof and new gable.

In 1898 the Carbondale National Bank succeeded the Jackson State Bank, of which Samuel W. Dunaway had been president. But Dunaway sold his interest, and when H. C. Mitchell became president in 1904, he moved the bank to North Illinois Avenue, changing the name to the Peoples National Bank of Carbondale, and then later to Carbondale National Bank. It began operation in 1905, with the board including W. W. Barr, W. W. Clemens, James M. Etherton, Dr. Mun Etherton, C. L. Ewing, F. M. Hewitt, F. T. Joyner, Dr. J. T. McAnally, Dr. H. C. Mitchell, Marcus H. Ogden,

Occasionally in the early 1900s companies made their own "money," as demonstrated by the $2.50 certificate from the Ohio and Mississippi Valley Telephone Company, in 1908.

The teller's cage in the First National Bank, when it was in its original building at 101 North Washington.

The First National Bank at 101 North Washington as it appeared in the 1920s.

and John R. Thorp. Joyner became president, but when he resigned in 1906, Dr. John S. Lewis took the position. The building it occupied at the northwest corner of Main and Illinois was three-storied, with Patten's drugstore on the first floor, offices on the second floor, and the Masons on the third floor. The bank renovated the building and used it until 1928, when it was torn down and a new building erected. In 1909 Dr. Lewis was succeeded as president by James M. Etherton. When he died in 1938, his son James Everett Etherton was made president. In 1971 he was followed by his son, William C. Etherton, who sold the bank in 1979.

Frank A. Prickett served as president of the First National Bank from 1893 to 1904, when William A. "Gus" Schwartz was named, with Judge Harker vice president, E. E. Mitchell cashier, W. H. Ashley assistant cashier, and J. E. Mitchell teller. Directors included Schwartz, Harker, Peters, E. E. Mitchell, and J. C. Hundley. Edward E. Mitchell took the president's position in 1913 and remained in it until 1936. In 1924 the First National Bank combined with the Carbondale Trust and Savings Bank, which William Schwartz had organized in 1897 at 110 North Illinois. James E. Mitchell was succeeded as president in 1947 by George N. Albon, who stayed in the position until 1960. In 1960 Walker Schwartz became president and served until 1968, when Glenn W. Storme was elected. He was followed in 1971 by Charles D. Renfro, who still serves.

The First National Bank building at 101 North Washington was remodelled twice, once in 1952 and again in 1960. In 1970 the bank moved to 509 South University, and in 1973, it was named the First National Bank and Trust of Carbondale. In 1991 the First National bank has seventy employees and an annual payroll of $1,250,000.

Until 1962 Carbondale had only two banking establishments, the First National Bank and the Carbondale National. But in that year the University

Staff at work in the bank.

The First National Bank at 101 North Washington, much later, with drive-through window.

Officially representing the bank at the open house, following the remodelling in 1952, this group, left to right: Tom Mofield, director; Charles Renfro (later president, from 1971 to present); Glenn W. Storme (president 1968 to 1971); Walker Schwartz (president 1960-1968); Clarence Wright and Robert Davis; George Albon (president 1947-1960).

Bank was organized, with a building at 1500 West Main, where it is still conducting business as First Bank. In 1970, a bank that had been chartered in Vergennes in 1919 was moved to the building at 101 N. Washington, which the First National Bank had vacated, and was named the Bank of Carbondale. In 1981 that bank moved to its present facility at 216 East Main. In 1985 a Gorham bank opened in Carbondale at 601 East Main under the name of City Bank of Carbondale, but in 1988 it merged with and became a branch of the City National Bank of Murphysboro. The 1991 yellow pages of the telephone directory list under banks a number of establishments that are actually chartered as savings and loan associations but which function as banks: Home Federal Savings and Loan (formerly the Carbondale Building and Loan Association and probably the oldest in Carbondale), Charter Bank (formerly the Carbondale Savings and Loan), the Chester Savings Bank, and the SIU Credit Union.

The First National Bank lobby as it appeared before 1950 at the North Washington facility.

The lobby of First National Bank and Trust in 1991.

The new First National Bank at 509 South University, as it appeared in 1971.

The First National Bank and Trust, as it appears in 1991.

The Carbondale National Bank lobby, remodelled in 1933. Left to right, J. M. Etherton, Georgia Sullivan, Dr. Monroe Etherton, F. M. Hewitt, Sr., J. E. Etherton, Willard Ottesen.

Carbondale National Bank, corner of Main and Illinois, as it appeared in 1928.

The Home Federal Savings and Loan, formerly the Carbondale Loan and Improvement Association, was originally established at 110 North Illinois. In the 1905 city directory, it was listed at that address, as was the Carbondale Trust and Savings Bank. George Schwartz, brother of W. A. Schwartz, was the secretary in 1905. The first board included Frank Clements, S. M. Compton, Hosea V. Ferrell, Samuel E. Harwood, T. K. Mackey, J. W. Miller, E. E. Mitchell, J. D. Peters, and E. K. Porter. In 1978 the location was changed to 635 East Walnut Street. This is a picture of that facility.

The Bank of Carbondale, 216 East Main.

# Carbondale Public Library

In 1921 a group of civic-minded women created the Carbondale Public Library, which was housed in the annex of the First Baptist Church (the Franklin Chapman house on West Main next to the church). Miss Julia Errett, the first librarian who remained until her retirement in 1937, was paid $1 a day. On May 15, 1922, a Library Board of Trustees was elected: Mrs. E. W. Reef, chairman; Mrs. T. A. Weaver, secretary; Mrs. A. F. Hooker, treasurer; Miss Mary Steagall; Mrs. A. D. Brubaker; Dr. H. W. Patterson; Judge A. L. Spiller; Commissioner Joe Anderson; and Prof. W. O. Brown.

This Board sought larger quarters and was given approval to use a room in the City Hall (on East Main Street), although the library patron had to walk through the courtroom to get to the library. In 1926 the Board bought the St. Andrews' Episcopal Church building at the corner of Elm and Normal, and Mrs. Samuel Harwood was appointed assistant to Miss Errett.

In 1937 Jack Spear became librarian, followed by Fern Brewer until 1942 when Mrs. Zella Rath was appointed. In 1951 Grace Burkett and her sister Anna left $30,000 to the library. Although the Library Board bought the John Lewis residence at 510 Walnut with the idea of converting it, the house was found not useable for a library and was sold in 1955, at which time the lot at 304 West Walnut was bought. A new building (cost $58,354) on this site (architects were Lee, Potter, Smith of Paducah and the builder was

This building on the southwest corner of Elm and University was first built to house the St. Andrew's Episcopal Church. The Library Board bought it in 1926 when the church moved to Mill Street. It served as the Carbondale Public Library until 1957, when the Library moved to Walnut Street. Currently the Unitarian Fellowship is using this building.

***Library Board Presidents:***
1922-52  Leah Reef
1952-66  Elmer Tuegel
1966-74  Ralph McCoy
1974-77  David Kenney
1977-81  Betty Mitchell
1981-85  Don Prosser
1985-89  Betty Mitchell
1989-91  Madelon Schilpp

The Library built in 1957 at 304 West Walnut Street.

Oakes Construction) was dedicated on October 4, 1957. The Board at that time were Elmer Tuegel, president; William Etherton, chairman of the Building Committee; Mrs. J. W. Barrow, secretary; Mrs. E. R. Sanders; Miss Dora Brubaker; Miss Jewell Truelove; Ted Ragsdale; and Dr. John Goff.

In 1953 Mrs. Leah Reef (who had been Library Board president from 1922 to 1952) left $38,000 to the library. By 1965 the facility was again inadequate, and various alternatives were explored. The Board acquired the Bradley house just west of the library to allow for expansion.

In January 1973 when Mrs. Rath retired, Charles Perdue was appointed head librarian. Between 1974 and 1977 the Board considered innumerable ways of funding a new library facility, including the possibility of combining the library with a new city hall. In December 1978 Mr. Perdue resigned, and Mr. Ray Campbell was hired as head librarian. Under his direction the Board renewed its interest in acquiring a new facility. After much effort the Board bought one half of the Brush School property in October 1980 from the Carbondale Elementary School District at a cost of $100,000 with an option to buy another quarter for $50,000 (which was done later). In November 1980 the Board asked the Carbondale City Council to approve a referendum for a new building; in December 1980 the Council gave its approval. The referendum (for $1,725,000) in February 1981 passed by a three-to-one margin.

In April 1982 ground was broken for the new building at 401 West Main, the Brush School site. The architect for the building was Harry Weese Associates. The library moved into the new building in July 1983.

The Bradley House at 306 West Oak was used as an annex for the library from 1965 to 1983.

The Public Library Board in 1981 when the referendum was passed for a new building on West Main Street: seated, left to right, George Black, Don Prosser, Eva Landecker, Mary Swindell, Don Vogler, Madelon Schilpp: standing: Mike Diamond, Betty Mitchell.

The Carbondale Public Library (West Main Street side), occupied in 1983, at 401 West Main (the old Brush School site).

# RECREATION

Parks, lakes, and clubs, rather than commercial ventures, have served recreational needs of Carbondale residents. Although little evidence exists of early parks, the town square itself formed a kind of park, and the entire atmosphere was rural. In the early 1900s people went south of town, to the area now known as Giant City State Park, to picnic and climb the rocks, long before facilities were there. In 1937 construction began on Crab Orchard Lake, which has served Carbondale and surrounding communities in a variety of recreational ways: swimming, camping, boating, and fishing. For a period of time the Southern Illinois Sail Club maintained a basin and provided much social activity at Crab Orchard.

In 1940 the Carbondale Park District, governed by five elected commissioners, was organized as a munici-

Going to the lake (Thompson Lake) are Mrs. J. W. Barrow and her children, Alice, Mary, and Jim in 1917.

Dr. J. W. Barrow at Thompson Lake, where he caught the fish.

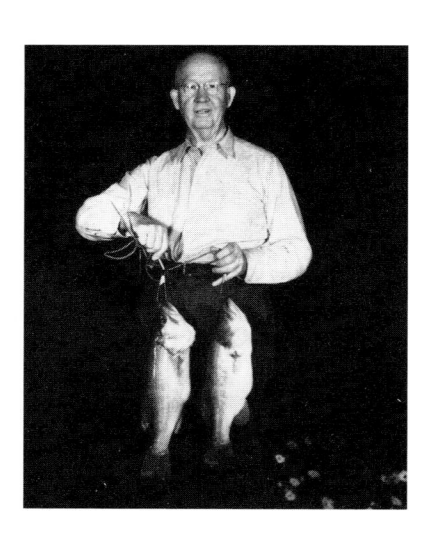

Bathing beauties at Thompson Lake in 1917: Alice Barrow and her friends.

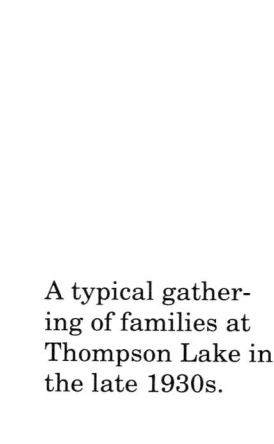

A typical gathering of families at Thompson Lake in the late 1930s.

pal corporation by the Illinois Park District Code. In 1941 the District established playgrounds at Attucks, Lincoln, and Springmore Schools, as well as a baseball diamond at the City Reservoir. In 1948 the District held swimming classes at Crab Orchard Lake, in 1950 hired a Recreation Director, Alan Domer, and in 1953 a Director, John T. Moake. In 1954, with help from civic groups and private contributions, City Park at the Reservoir Lake was built. Since then, the District has improved the park and changed the name to Evergreen Park. It has also built a small park at the corner of West Main and Glenview, Turley Park; has built Oakdale Park on North Oakland; with Junior Sports, has provided Doug Lee Park on East Grand; has acquired the YMCA facility on Sunset (housing the LIFE Community Center and the Alice Wright Day Care Center) and has added soccer fields; with the school district has created playgrounds at Winkler, Lewis, Parrish, and Thomas Schools; and has established administrative offices at Hickory Lodge (1115 West Sycamore) and maintenance facilities in the Howell Building (West Main), through private donations. The Park District has sponsored the Special Olympics for a number of years.

Private clubs have served Carbondale: Midland Hills Golf Club, at one time a favorite of many, provided space for cottages on a deep lake, as well as golf, swimming, and fishing. The Jackson Country Club caters primarily to golfers, but provides a pool and clubhouse. Thompson Lake, with cabins, swimming, and boating, was closer to the community and another favorite place to get away from the heat during the hot summers.

Professor Bill Marberry, in the Department of Botany at SIU and a native of Carbondale, created an arboretum on Wall Street at Pleasant Hill Road in the early 1940s and contributed it to the Park District in 1987.

Giant City (Makanda, IL) in 1911: a typical rock formation there at that time and still attracting people constantly.

The same group, same day, at Giant City, becoming a bit bolder.

Also at Giant City, 1911, with a pony as the main attraction.

Interior of Giant City Lodge.

# GIANT CITY

Giant City State Park has been a favorite recreation spot for generations. In addition to the lodge, pictured here, are cabins, shelters, play areas, trails, and rocks for climbing. The lodge was built in the early 1930s by the CCC. In recent years it has been renovated and added onto. It now houses a large dining room in addition to smaller dining rooms.

Giant City Lodge, ca. early 1940s.

Betty Berry and Harry Lutz on the bridge at Midland Hills in the late 1930s.

A clubhouse at Midland Hills in the 1930s.

Women at a picnic in the early 1900s at Midland Hills, which became a much used area for swimming, fishing, boating, and golf.

Crab Orchard spillway in 1956: used extensively by Carbondale residents and SIU students, from March to October. Photo 1956.

Early Park District Board, meeting at Tom Langdon's: from left to right, Jerry W. Lottmann, Alicia Schneider, Frank Bridges, Tom Langdon, W. A. Howe, Oscar Atherton.

Hickory Lodge, 1115 W. Sycamore, formerly the Martin house.

Gazebo at Turley Park, Glenview and Main.

Playground at Turley Park.

Oakdale Park, North Oakland Avenue.

Above left: Special Olympics, sponsored by the Park District, held annually at McAndrew Stadium.

Above: Participants in Special Olympics.

Left: A race in the Special Olympics.

One function of the Park District is to sponsor sports activities for all ages. The Jets pictured here won the Baseball Khoury League in 1957, coached by Tom Langdon.

111

# Medical Facilities

From the beginning Carbondale has been blessed with an adequate number of doctors. According to Wright, *The Carbondale Transcript* on July 16, 1857, gave an informal census taken by Asgill Conner, and that census listed five doctors; by 1870 the number had raised to nine plus a dentist, and in 1880 to ten.

The Keeley Institute was established in 1891 in the former home of William J. Allen, which had been lived in more recently by Dr. John Salter. The site was six acres, from Illinois Avenue to University in the 600 block. Wright cites John Lethem, ". . . Dr. W. O. Young, who was resident medical director for the institute in Carbondale, lived with his family in the headquarters building, and there was room to accommodate about seventeen patients. Townspeople were asked to cooperate with the institute by supplying additional accommodations. Dr. Young, a graduate of Bellevue University in New York, had been a very successful practicing physician before his connection with the institute and was completely convinced of the benefits derived from the cure. Just when, and just why, the institute branch in Carbondale closed is not definitely known." John W. D. Wright speculated that reasons may have been the increased activity of the Women's Christian Temperance Union, (organized in 1888) which worked on preventing drunkenness, and the return of saloons in Carbondale in the middle 1890s. The Will Hewitts bought the property for a home, and then Dr. John S. Lewis, Sr., purchased it and lived in it. In 1912 Dr. Lewis converted it for a brief period to the Amy Lewis Hospital, which he ran with Dr. Roscoe Lewis and Dr. J. W. Barrow. However, these doctors were not basically interested in operating a hospital, and Dr. Roscoe Lewis, who then owned it, gave the building and grounds to two Methodist Church groups: The Women's Society for Christian Service and the local Methodist Church.

In 1916 Mrs. Holden gave $40,000 for an addition on the stipulation that it be named Holden Hospital. It was expanded in 1922 and again in 1942, but it closed in 1953 and was demolished in 1976.

The Keeley Institute, 600 block of South Illinois and South University, was established in 1891. Around 1900 Dr. John S. Lewis, Sr., purchased the house for a home, but he turned it into the Amy Lewis Hospital in 1912-13.

The above house was expanded in 1922, was renamed Holden Hospital, and was further expanded in 1942. It was demolished in 1976.

# CARBONDALE CLINIC

Dr. James W. Barrow (1874-1961) came to Carbondale in 1910 and began to practice medicine. His office was in the Neber Building, second floor, at 211 South Illinois Avenue. In 1938 he was joined by his son-in-law Dr. Leo J. Brown. In 1939 Dr. John S. Lewis, Jr., joined them, and in 1940 the practice moved to a new facility at 308 South Illinois, at which time Dr. Jack Taylor joined them.

According to Dr. Leo Brown's "The Carbondale Clinic," "The Medical Community of Carbondale 1938-42 consisted of the following doctors: Officing over the Hub Cafe building was Dr. Zeb Carmen. . . . There were several doctors officing over the Hewitt Drug Store. Dr. Ben Fox. . . Dr. William Felts. . . Dr. Ellis Crandle. . . . Dr. C. H. Moss had a small office across the street from the Methodist Church on Main Street. On North Illinois in the Virginia Building were the offices of Dr. W. A. Brandon and Dr. Fred Lingle. . . . Dr. Clyde Brooks also had his office over the Hub Cafe. . . . Dr. Jewel Bass was a black physician who had an office on the east side of Carbondale. . . . Dr. John Lewis officed over the Hub Cafe. Doctors Monroe and Fred Etherton officed over Hewitt's Drug Store and had most of the Railroad, Industrial, and Insurance Practice in Carbondale."

World War II took most of the doctors away from Carbondale, but there was a sufficient number of older doctors to care for the population. After the war, a number of young doctors joined the Clinic: Dan Foley, Eli Borkon, William Cassell. Dr. Jack Barrow, son of Dr. J. W. Barrow, also was part of the group. Problems at Holden Hospital led to Dr. John S. Lewis' purchasing property at 404 and 406 West Main (the group of Barrow, Brown, Lewis, and Taylor had operated the Herrin Hospital from 1946 to 1949). Thus, in 1949 the Southern Illinois Hospital Corporation began as a not-for-profit, and in 1950 opened Doctors Hospital (now known as Memorial Hospital). The Carbondale Clinic occupied the first floor of the facility at 406 West Main from 1950 to 1967. Then it moved to 2601 West Main, where it is at present.

The first facility (left side of photo) built for the Carbondale Clinic, at 211-1/2 South Illinois Avenue, used from 1939 to 1950.

Nurse Ruth Kenney in 1955, holding one of the 15,000 babies she handled in Holden and Memorial Hospitals.

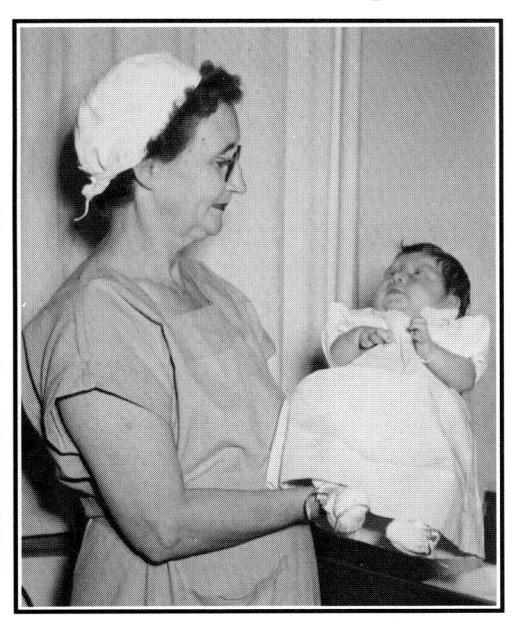

In 1952, ground breaking for the new wing of Doctor's Hospital at 404 West Main: left to right: doctors J. W. Barrow, Dan Foley, John B. Taylor, John S. Lewis, Charles Fildes, Leo J. Brown, and Jack Barrow.

# THE FOUNDERS OF THE CARBONDALE CLINIC

**Dr. John S. Lewis, Jr.**

**Dr. J. W. Barrow**

**Dr. Leo J. Brown**

**Dr. Jack Taylor**

The Carbondale Clinic when it was housed at Doctors Hospital (now Carbondale Memorial), from 1950 to 1967.

The current Carbondale Clinic at 2601 West Main Street.

An aerial view of Memorial Hospital, before the addition of the Cancer Treatment Center on the east.

From Jackson Street, a view of Memorial Hospital after the enclosure of the entrance and walkway, in addition to the new east wing for cancer treatment.

# SOCIAL LIFE

Clubs and organizations have been prevalent in Carbondale throughout its history. The Normal School provided programs from its earliest days, by the Zetetic and Socratic Societies, which offered entertainment both in Old Main and in the Opera House. According to Wright, "These societies, in turn, provided the impetus that led, in 1896, to the establishment of the Cosmopolitan Literary Club of Carbondale for the ladies of the town which in time became the Carbondale Woman's Club." Charter members included both faculty wives and townswomen.

In "Carbondale Remembered" Julia Mitchell Etherton gives a report, "In 1900 some of the neighborhood women formed the Oak Street circle which is still in existence and meets monthly." After naming the members in 1903 she wrote, "The group held an annual masquerade party on Halloween night with guests, one of the social events of the year. The idea of the annual Halloween Mardi gras parade held in Carbondale for many years until the late 1920's originated with this group. . . ."

A Year Book of The Home Culture Club for 1917-18 indicates that it was organized in 1914 by Mrs. Ada D. Caldwell and that it met fortnightly. Of the various programs, a sampling ranges from "Composition and nutritive value of eggs to the body" and "Ways of serving eggs" to "Foods for the professional man" and "Foods for the out-of-doors man."

A second Carbondale Woman's Club was organized in 1921, as part of the Federation of Woman's Clubs, and ultimately came to be known as the Carbondale Federated Woman's Club. A 1937-38 Year Book reveals programs based on literature and art, conservation and garden, education, music, and American home. Mrs. John I. Wright was president in 1937-38. The 1944-45 Year Book shows different interests: Child study, home, literature and arts. The projects for that year included community chest, cancer control, student loan, Red Cross, polio fund, Student Christian Foundation, Indian Welfare, to name a few.

Other groups have formed over the years, some more organized than others: Beta Sigma Phi, the PEO, Carbondale City Panhellenic, Business and Professional Women, not to mention rug clubs, sewing clubs, and bridge clubs by the dozens. An early Camera Club provided a competition for amateur photographers.

Five garden clubs for women developed over the years; the Carbondale Garden Club, the first, was organized in 1929, followed by the Carbondale Garden Study Club in 1933, then The Evergreen Garden Club in 1947. Next was the Amateur Garden Club in 1948 and the last, the Egyptian Garden Club, in 1949. In 1951 these five formed a Council of Garden Clubs. Over the years, these groups have sponsored flower shows, beautification projects, schools on flower arranging, programs, and lectures, and have generally contributed to the aesthetics of Carbondale. In 1942, for instance, the existing groups sponsored a magnolia tree planting project, planting over a hundred trees to beautify the city.

The men also organized into groups, ranging from social and philanthropic to community service. Some of these include the Masons, the Elks, the American Legion, Veterans of Foreign Wars, the Moose, the Eagles, the IOOF, as well as the Rotary, the Lions, the Kiwanis, and the Jaycees. One of the earliest was the Shekinah Lodge No. 241, which met in 1857 in an upstairs room at 118 South Illinois. The Odd Fellows Lodge shared the room, with each group paying a yearly rental of $38.00. In 1864 the Masons moved to the third floor of the northwest corner of Main and Illinois. Early masters from 1857 to 1866 were Isaac Mulkey, William S. Mason, William S. Post, William Standing, Robert H. Marron, Isaac Rapp, Richard Dudding, and William Richart. In 1914 when the Carbondale City Hall was built on the corner of East Main and North Marion, the Masons contributed $9,000 and received a ninety-nine year lease allowing them to use the third floor. In 1961 they built a new facility at 1510 West Sycamore.

The Carbondale Elks Club, BPOE #1243, was chartered in 1911 with fifty-six members. The group soon began to raise money to buy the Dr. Keesee property, at 220 West Jackson, and in 1914-15 built the original part of the building at a reported cost of $30,000 or more. In the

One common form of social life for women in the late 1940s and throughout the 1950s was the rug club. These ladies in 1948 are hooking a rug in Jean Smith Foley's living room: standing, left to right, Mary Smith, Maude Daniels, Lucy Phillips, Dora Anderson. Sitting, ? , Constance Stotlar, Lillian Warren, Mabel Taylor, and Ada Keene.

late 1940s, with G. Nyle Huffman as chairman of the Building Committee, the Elks Club started making plans for adding on to the building a one-story addition to the east.

Service clubs, primarily for men at the beginning, had their start in the early 1920s. The Carbondale Rotary Club had twenty-two charter members in 1920. Activities over the years have included a loan fund for SIU students, cooperation with International Rotary exchange programs, safety plaques for area businesses and industries, academic awards for high school students, and United Fund. The Carbondale Lions Club, chartered in 1921 with fifty-two men, has supported the State Program for the Blind and many community projects, including establishing a mosquito abatement district (the first in the United States); preventing Piles Fork Creek from flooding; building seven shelters at the City Reservoir Park; building the press box at the high school football field; providing street signs for the city streets for eleven years; providing the first radar equipment for the city police; clearing the beach at the Girl Scout Camp Cedar Point at Little Grassy Lake; collecting 15,000 (to date) used eye glasses for people in South America; supplying eye glasses for school children in Carbondale; and since 1968 providing the fireworks at the Abe Martin baseball field for the community on the Fourth of July. Among fund raisers to support these projects have been broom sales, pancake days, rummage sales, providing lunch for visiting high school bands at homecoming, and more recently painting the city fire plugs. The Kiwanis Club organized in 1948, and has since organized another group that meets in the morning. Projects have included the annual "Kids Day," a national event when the members sell peanuts to benefit children's funds. They also hold a pancake day in the spring and contribute to a variety of local children's groups.

---

The Home Culture Club sponsored a variety of programs. In 1918 the club celebrated Washington's birthday: bottom, left to right, Trix Albon, Mary Smith, Grace Young, Mildred Ismert; top, Jenny Feirich, Stella Scott, Ruby Gullett, Nettie Spiller.

The Carbondale Woman's Club gathered for a photograph in 1990: first row, left to right: Mary Brown, Barbara Doherty, Barbara Kimmel, Marguerite Robinson, Jean Foley, Dorothy Vogler, Helen Foster, Rene Potter; second row: Jane Pulley, Ernie Fichtel, Maude Tenney, Trish Medlin, Mary Wright, Bonnie Moreno, Mary Simon, Dorothy Morris, Mary Swindell, Dottie Prosser, Diane Dorsey, Ginnie Neal, Katie Simond, Mary Alice Kimmel.

Among the functions of the Carbondale Woman's Club was sponsorship of the Halloween activities in Carbondale. Featured here is the 1928 Halloween Queen, Alice Patterson.

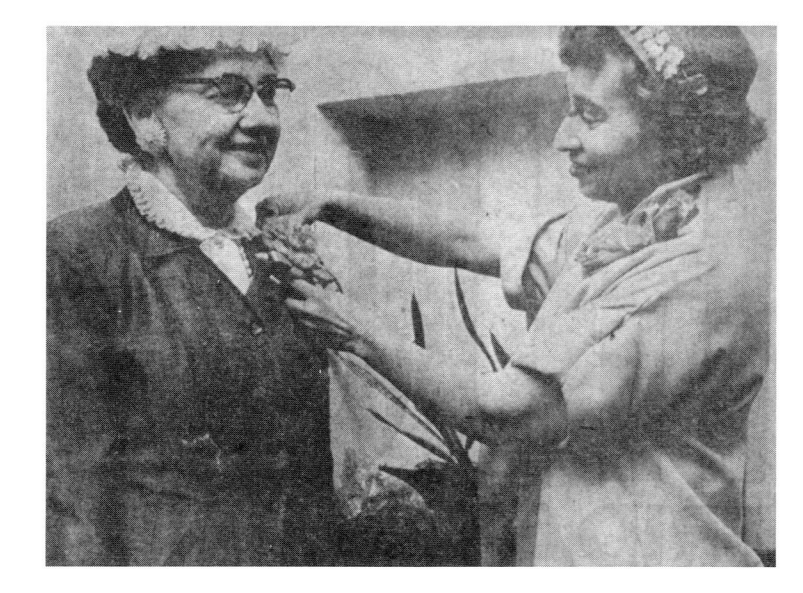

The Illinois Federation of Women's Clubs at its convention honored Mrs. Elbert Fulkerson of Carbondale, who had been named as Illinois Mother of the Year. Pinning a corsage on her is Mrs. Tom Langdon.

Also popular among women's groups were the garden clubs of Carbondale. Pictured here in 1950 in the garden of Mrs. E. G. Lentz: first row, Mrs. Clyde Woods, Mrs. Chalmer Gross, Mrs. J. W. Barrow, Mrs. Madge Sanders, Lucy K. Woody; top, Mrs. Lutz, Mrs. S. E. Boomer, Mrs. G. L. Bradley, Mrs. E. M. Thrailkill, Mrs. Eva McIntosh, Mrs. Maude Daniel, Emma Bowyer, Mrs. H. J. Patterson, Mrs. F. Cox, Mrs. C. Fox, Mrs. Lilian Bundy.

118

Community sororities, such as the Beta Sigma Phi group shown here, also commanded the attention of Carbondale women. Bottom, left to right: Edna Medlin, Lillian Hayes, Ladaw Bridges, Liz Lewis, Mary Mars. Standing: Jean Gladders, Tid Stroup, Chick Hayes, Jerry Taylor, Helen Gilbert, Lee Phelps, Jean Foley, Dorothy Strohman.

People interested in photography formed groups as well. In 1949 the Carbondale Camera Club is shown in the basement of the Roberts Hotel.

119

THE ELKS MAGAZINE STUDEBAKER
GOOD WILL TOUR
WASHINGTON D.C. TO KANSAS CITY
THE ELKS NATIONAL CONVENTION
JULY 16
Firestone
FIRST CHOICE OF CHAMPIONS
GLOBE
BATTERY
EQUIPPED

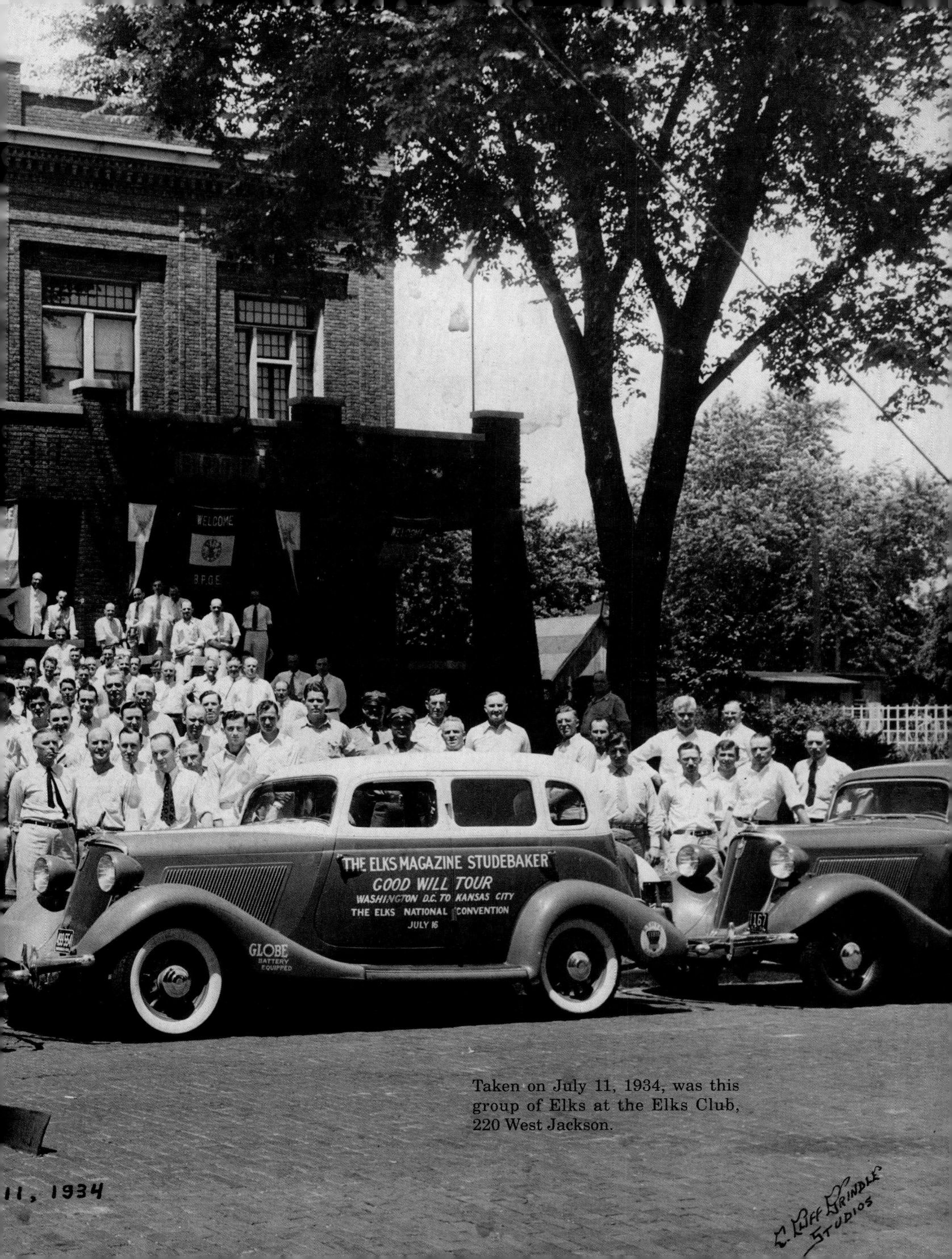

Taken on July 11, 1934, was this group of Elks at the Elks Club, 220 West Jackson.

An Elks' team in the late 1930s. Front, left to right, River Hewitt, Randall Fichtel, Walker Schwartz; back, ? , ? , Winton Walkup, Marvin Muckelroy, George Albon.

An Elks' float for a parade, late 1930s.

The current Elks' building, 220 West Jackson.

One of the fund raisers by the Lions Club is the Pancake Day. Shown here in 1967 are Hans Fischer, an unidentified customer, Robert Odaniell, Jerry Levelsmeier, Roger Spear, and in the foreground, David Kenney. The Club bought the pancake machine, which rotates, from a man in Zion, Illinois.

The Lions Club in 1949.

Girl Scout and Boy Scout troops abound in Carbondale. Pictured are Eagle Scouts, from Troop 70, in 1964: Dick Langdon, Tom Langdon, Terry McDaniel, Jon Swanson.

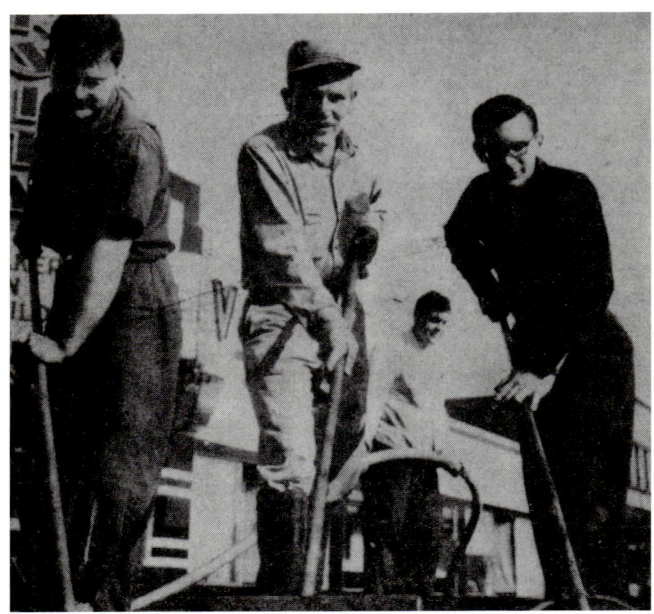

In 1955 the Carbondale Junior Chamber Commerce participated in a "clean up Carbondale" campaign. Shown are Tom Langdon, Chuck Rathjen, and Larry Doyle.

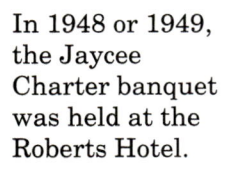

In 1948 or 1949, the Jaycee Charter banquet was held at the Roberts Hotel.

# Chapter V

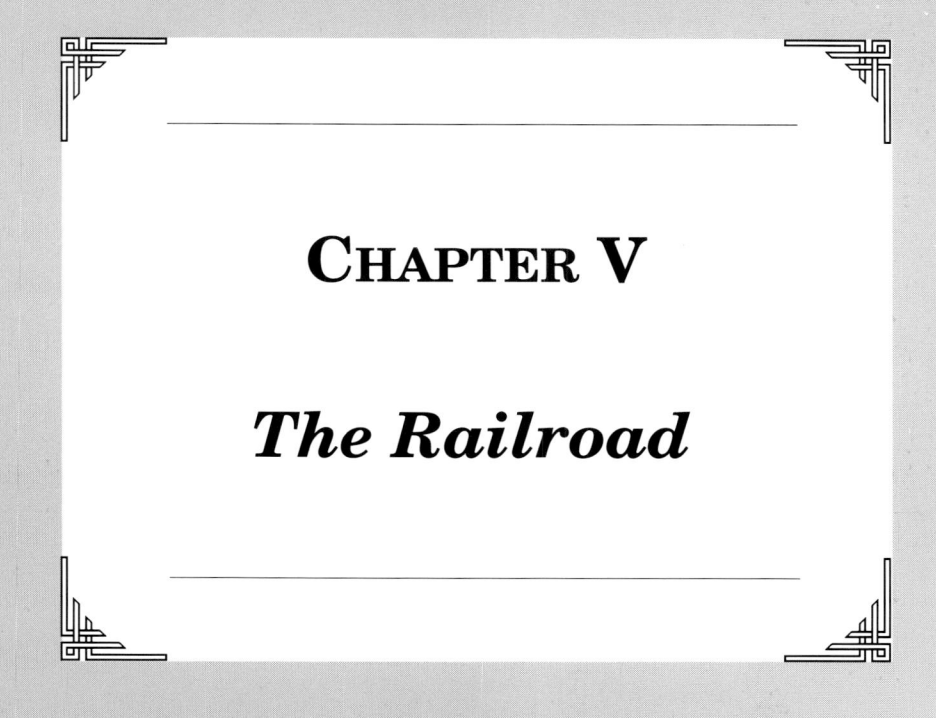

## *The Railroad*

125

From Brush's own recount the railroad played a central role in the beginning of Carbondale. Before he found the stakes, however, the railroad had to have been in existence. According to Stover, "During the year 1850-51 the Illinois Central Railroad came into existence as the result of a generous land grand from the federal government. The land grant legislation of 1850 marked the first time that public lands from the national government were to be used directly to help the private construction of a major rail line. Thus, a precedent was established that was to greatly influence nearly all railroad construction in the West for the next generation. The very size of the Illinois Central was unusual. When the 700 miles of charter line in the state were finished in 1856, the Illinois Central was probably the longest railroad in the world." He went on, "It was rather strange that such a railroad should appear in a region as far west as Illinois at midcentury.

... On the eve of the Civil War, the five states of the old Northwest alone could claim 32 percent of the national rail mileage, and Illinois, with 2,790 miles, was second in mileage in the nation, bested only by 2,946 miles in Ohio." Stover also reported, "The charter of the Illinois Central had had several significant provisions added before its final approval by the Illinois legislature. The company was required to complete its mail line from Cairo northwest to the Mississippi River within four years, and its eastern branch to Chicago within six years." The charter lines were completed between December 23, 1851 and September 27, 1856—a monumental task.

Brush's own words (cited in Chapter I) relate the arrival of the first train in Carbondale. In the words of another, William K. Ackerman, a twenty-two year old New Yorker who worked for the railroad, "... the people of 'Egypt' (southern Illinois below St. Louis) [note that even then the area was referred to as Egypt] had: 'turned out to witness the novel sight, to them, of a locomotive engine and train of cars. They lined the track on both sides at every station, the men dressed in their snuff-colored jeans, and the women with gaudy-colored calicoes, check aprons and big sun-bonnets. They stood in dumb amazement.'"

But the Illinois Central was not the only railroad important to the early development and history of Carbondale. Wright points out, "Another boost for Carbondale's economy during this period [late1870s] came from its increasing importance as a transportation center, due to its location on the Illinois Central line. In about 1870 the Carbondale and Shawneetown Railroad was incorporated by a group of coal operators from the east. . . . The Carbondale to Marion section of this road had been completed by January, 1872. In addition to carrying coal from the mines near Carterville and elsewhere in Williamson County to Carbondale, it brought cotton, tobacco, and dried fruits for reshipment on the Illinois Central. Edmund Newsome comments on the fact that with the operation of this line one conspicuous feature of early Carbondale disappeared. This was the long trains of wagons that formerly made their way westward on Main Street to the railroad station, each carrying a single large hogshead of tobacco." In addition, a railroad line was built from Mt. Carbon to Carbondale.

By 1880, the Illinois Central had employed R. J. Cavett as superintendent of engineers, conductors, brakemen, and telegraph operators, twenty or more altogether, making the railroad payroll a factor in the economy of Carbondale at that time. In 1882 the Grand Tower and Carbondale Railroad Company was incorporated; it bought the railroad line from Grand Tower to Carbondale and built a depot north of Carbondale, called the Mt. Carbon Depot. According to Wright, ". . . its principal function was the delivery of coal and coke from Jackson and Williamson County sources to the river area. This railroad was one of the lines which eventually found its way into the possession of the Illinois Central when it put together the network of feeder lines which were to be a big benefit to Carbondale in the following decade."

Wright notes that ". . . in 1880 the first stage of a line from Carbondale to Pinckneyville was built, going as far as Harrison, north of Murphysboro. The Pinckneyville end of the line was built about a year later. There were also lines form St. Louis penetrating Southern Illinois at different points. . . . Southern Illinois coal, grain, and other farm and industrial products began to come through Carbondale in increasing volume. This was a trend which would pick up substantially in 1895 when the Illinois Central acquired all of these feeder lines on a ninety-nine year lease."

Maycock reports, "In 1882 the Illinois Central, after years of negotiations, acquired a four-hundred-year lease to the railroads between Cairo and New Orleans and standardized the gauge on the entire length of this route. For the first time trains could run directly from Chicago to New Orleans without changing tracks or gauges. In Carbondale shipments of coal as well as local produce and manufactured goods resumed on a large scale. Flour and grain shipments were particularly important, and in 1882 the Illinois Central constructed a special siding on the east side of town to accommodate the three principal flour mills."

The Illinois Central, after problems of a Pullman strike in 1894 and an epidemic of yellow fever in 1897, nevertheless put money into the railroad facilities at Carbondale. As a result many railroad families and workers were transferred to Carbondale. Maycock reports, "Not surprisingly, railroad improvements dominated the life of the town throughout the year [1898]. By June more than seventy-five men were at work constructing the brick roundhouse, railroad water tank, artesian well, and seven new switches to handle the large number of freight trains slated to be dispatched from Carbondale. George B. Swift Company of Chicago, specializing in railroad buildings, erected a roundhouse that initially held nine engines. Within a few months of completion it was expanded to accommodate an additional nine. The artesian well and commodious water tower made Carbondale the chief watering station in the area, while the abundance of Southern Illinois coal and greatly expanded loading chute made this a major coaling point for Illinois Central trains. Railroad schedules published in 1898 show at least thirty-three trains a day on five different lines stopping in Carbondale, and this number increased over the next few years as facilities expanded even further."

In 1899 the Illinois Central built new offices for the St.

Louis Division and consolidated its operation from nearby towns to Carbondale. To improve the aesthetics of the Division Office (northeast corner of the town square), the Illinois Central created a park setting, with a fountain and plantings. This building was expanded in 1914 and in 1922. With such expansion, more railroad employees were moved to Carbondale. By 1905 the railroad was reported to have thirty passenger and fifty freight trains daily, with over three hundred local employees and an annual payroll of $264,000. Part of this number no doubt was the result of the mail service being transferred from Cairo to Carbondale in 1903.

Stover comments on the Illinois Central after the turn of the century: "The relative decline that came to railroad traffic in the first generation of the new century hit the passenger business before the freight. Between the years 1900 and 1926, I. C. freight revenue increased almost sixfold, from $24.8 million to $145 million. In the same twenty-five year period passenger revenue on the I. C. expanded not quite fourfold, from $7.3 million to $28.2 million. Put another way in 1900-1901 the freight business was about three and a half times as large as the passenger traffic; whereas twenty-five years later freight traffic produced more than five times as much revenue as passenger travel. Of the modes of transport the most serious threat to rail passenger traffic in the first decades of the new century came from the electric interurban and the private automobile."

Shortages during WW I faced the railroad as well as other segments. But in 1912, the *Panama Limited*—a new all-pullman train that ran between Chicago and New Orleans in twenty-three hours—made its debut. This deluxe train was especially known for its dining-car service. During the war freight traffic increased by more than ten percent, although passenger service was cut back. The federal government, under President Wilson, had taken over all railroads during the war, but in the spring of 1920 they were returned to private management.

During the 1920s the Illinois Central prospered, and Carbondale prospered with it. The railroad was buying new equipment and making improvements. Most of the traffic increase in the 1920s was in shipping bituminous coal from southern Illinois mines and fruits and vegetables from southern Illinois farms. Between 1912 and 1929 the Illinois Central increased the number of coal cars by 45 percent, although in the late 1920s the automobile was taking its toll on passenger traffic. The depression between 1927 and 1932 hit the Illinois Central hard, as it did all the nation. Coal mines in southern Illinois closed, and people lacked the money to use the railway. Some employees of the railroad were out of jobs, and some of those who remained employed were asked to take a cut in pay.

The Emergency Railroad Transportation Act, in 1933, attempted to boost the economy of the railroad, and indeed a slight upward trend followed. And the Chicago "Century of Progress" exposition in 1933 and 1934 increased passenger traffic on the Illinois Central. In the late 1930s, however, freight traffic began to decline as the result of paved highways (more freight was being carried by trucks) and of air travel. The railroad's answer was improved service, with air-conditioned passenger cars, brightly colored trains, and faster rail service.

During WW II the railroads played a great part in transporting troops and goods, with the result of greatly increased traffic in both areas. At the same time, steam locomotives were being replaced by diesel locomotives. Figures from the war years reveal the increases: from 1939 to 1945, freight revenue of the Illinois Central doubled, while passenger revenue quadrupled.

In 1943 the Illinois Central initiated a program to train young men between sixteen and seventeen to become firemen, brakemen, flagmen, and switchmen. The assistant general manager, Wayne A. Johnston, was responsible for recruiting and for the training program, which was set up in Carbondale. Many of the recruits were from families of Illinois Central employees. These young people helped the railroad during the war (while many employees were part of the military) and remained with the railroad after the war.

Throughout these years the economy of Carbondale followed that of the nation; certainly the Illinois Central had a major impact on that economy. During the war many families moved to Carbondale in order to work for the Illinois Central out of the St. Louis Division Office located here. In 1947 the *City of New Orleans* made its first run, from Chicago to New Orleans, in less than sixteen hours. After the war, however, the importance of the railroad to the Carbondale economy began to decline.

Wayne Johnston, the first native of Illinois to head the Illinois Central, became president in 1945 and stayed in the office until 1966. But a decline in the railroad in these years was inevitable. In 1951 the Illinois Central celebrated its 100th anniversary. Between 1951 and 1952 the St. Louis Division showed an increase in fruit cars of 113 percent. In 1952, when Carbondale had a population of 15,000, 619 were on the Illinois Central payroll, which was $2,435,290 that year. The principal shippers at that time were Kroger, Koppers (which had bought the Ayer and Lord Tie Company), Triangle Construction, Martin Oil, Hill Produce, Illinois Fruit Growers, and Colp Lumber.

In 1958 when Harry Koonce took over as trainmaster at Carbondale, there were 58 freight trains and 20 passenger trains daily. In 1966 Koonce recalls that the Illinois Central's St. Louis Division Office had 2700 employees with an annual budget of fifteen million dollars. By 1961 the shift to diesel power was complete, making coal to power the locomotives no longer needed and resulting in less coal being shipped through Carbondale.

In 1982, on September 1, the Division Office closed in Carbondale, but by then the University had certainly taken over as the major industry in Carbondale.

# Depot

Almost certainly not the first passenger facility in Carbondale, this is the station as it existed in 1885. Its location is not precisely known although there is indication that it stood across the tracks from the present depot; among railroad people, it was almost always referred to as "the depot." This building was replaced by the current brick structure in 1893. That station, in turn, was replaced by the present Amtrak station in 1978. The new Amtrak building was constructed farther from the street grade crossings in order to minimize motor traffic interference by standing passenger trains.

Carbondale's spanking new station, opened just after the turn of the century, provided the citizens of Southern Illinois with easy access to the rest of America and the World. Fast trains to Chicago, St. Louis, Memphis, and New Orleans were available several times each day, as were other easy connections both east and west.

A crack Illinois Central passenger train, perhaps the *Panama Limited, City of Miami,* or other racehorse of the Mainline of Mid-America, poised for the last leg of its journey from the Caribbean or the Gulf to the Great lakes. On the near end of the station can be seen the Van Noys Restaurant, now sadly gone. The Van Noys was a popular meeting place for coffee and sandwiches after a night at one of Carbondale's many lively night spots. The watchman, who guarded the crossing against the dozens of daily trains, both passenger and freight, spent his free minutes in a shack just out of the picture to the right.

To the extreme right can be seen another Carbondale landmark, the Green Mill Restaurant, with its model mill spinning its vanes above the front door.

The rear view of the station, looking south along Illinois Avenue. The dark building to the left was Leo's Tavern, a popular watering place for waiting passengers — and sometimes train crew — and the light building to the right is the Prince Hotel, destroyed by fire.

The ticket office of the Carbondale I.C. Station. From this point, the people of Carbondale left to visit relatives in Paducah or Centralia, journeyed to the Century of Progress in Chicago, or set off for an afternoon in Sportsman's park in St. Louis. Or, clad in khaki or navy blue, said goodbye to loved ones and set off for one of the Great Wars.

One of the earliest types of locomotives used on the I. C. While the first four engines on the Company's books were *Betsy, Roxy, Mary Ann,* and *Union,* it is thought that the company also had four secondhand locomotives named *Bee* (later *Cairo*), *Medford, Pilot,* and *Rogers.* It's not unreasonable to suppose that the engine barged down the Ohio River to begin building the road from the southern end was renamed *Cairo,* and therefore that it was the splendid locomotive that saluted Carbondale on that grand 4th of July in 1854.

The introduction of sleeping cars on the Illinois Central in 1856 marked a great step forward in passenger comfort. This car, among the first on the system, was in use a year later.

Over the railroad's history countless "big spenders" have attached their private cars to crack Illinois Central trains for luxurious travel to the exciting cities on the system. This, one of the most elegant of the private "varnish," boasts an ornate filigreed rear platform, gilded devices on the sides, and leaded glass windows.

130

Any observation car worthy of the name was fitted with a polished brass railing surrounding the rear platform. This one is among the fanciest!

Early railroad passengers were treated to the most elegant in wooden coach work and gilded decoration. These coaches, dating from the late 1800s, were among the first to be equipped with closed vestibules as opposed to dangerous open platforms.

The view from the observation car — the quickly receding countryside and the envious waves from the children alongside the track — is often our most cherished memory of early railroading.

This first class day coach of the late decades of the 19th century wasn't lavishly decorated but provided most of the comforts that travelers enjoyed well into the nineteen hundreds. The notable exception was the lighting, here oil lamps and later a gas system. Although they provided as much illumination as most travelers of the day were accustomed to, a wreck involving the wooden coaches almost always resulted in a serious fire. Equipping the coaches with electricity later in the century increased the safety of rail travel immensely.

An earlier, and certainly more austere, sleeping car interior. Like the later cars, the upper berths were formed by pulling down the panels, while the seat cushions were shifted to form the lowers.

A late-19th-century sleeping car made up for daylight traveling. For night time use, each decorative overhead panel was lowered to form the upper berth, as can be seen in the background. The seat cushions were then rearranged to form the lowers. The patterns shown on the panels were intricate and elaborate hand inlaid marquetry, the labor of hundreds of European artisans imported by the Pullman Company for this and other decorative work on the Pullman fleet.

The steam switch engine, shown here at the tie plant, scurried around Carbondale's freight and passenger yards cutting out cars from the main-line to St. Louis assignments, rear-ranging passenger consists, and doing whatever was necessary to see that the right car got to the right place. These men, in the early days of the century, are unidentified except for Roy Gregory of South Washington Street, third from left.

Even with the best of care and equipment — and the best of men — accidents still happened. This old print shows a fairly serious passenger train wreck a little south of Carbondale in 1909.

Although almost all traces are now gone, there used to be a lively trolley business between Carbondale and Murphysboro. Its local terminal was the now-demolished Franklin Hotel.

The *Thunderbolt Express* shown here in 1892 was the first all-strawberry express train in the country. It began operation in 1867, rushing the iced fruit from southern Illinois to Chicago. The fast expresses carrying bananas from New Orleans, peaches from southern Illinois as well as the strawberries were often *highballed* — given priority — over all but the most important passenger trains. The old ice plant, still in use but not producing ice, provided hundred-pound blocks of clear ice for countless thousands of such trains over the years.

The home away from home for the crew of a freight train. This early 20th century caboose featured oil lamps, a coal-fired pot bellied stove, and a desk for the "skipper" — the conductor — including even a swivel chair. The bright glow in the center of the picture came from the windows of the cupola, arranged so a crewman could overlook the entire train, spotting trouble before it got out of hand.

A contingent of Woodsmen of the World (Modern Woodsmen?) prepare for an official journey in 1883. The photo, taken from atop a boxcar spotted by the freight station, is from a popular postcard of that year.

Station at Brahms
Carbondale, Colorado

# Dining Cars

A giant step in American railroading occurred in 1867 with the introduction of Pullman's "Hotel Car," a sleeper which, with a kitchen installed at one end, doubled as a dining car. The menu on a diner of the 19th century might include a half-dozen meat dishes including beef roasts and steaks to order, three or four game dishes including, perhaps, a roast turkey and venison. All this accompanied by fresh fish, a half dozen vegetables, and an assortment of desserts — all produced from raw products on the train. Nineteenth century voyagers might find themselves paying up to seventy-five cents for such a meal. Most important railroads prided themselves on dining car specialties, perhaps crab or other seafood from the Atlantic seaboard railroads or game specialties from the Western lines. The I. C., particularly the *Panama,* was known throughout the traveling world for its New Orleans cuisine and its real specialty, French Toast. The normally lavish liquor service on a diner or parlor car was a stop and go affair, depending on the jurisdiction the train was travelling through. Carbondale was dry well into the twentieth century.

Dining cars, this one built around 1890, surely kept pace with sleeping cars in terms of luxury and elegance. And speed! While most trains of the day were locals, making every stop along the way for passengers, freight, milk, and even crates of baby chicks, the crack passenger "varnish" — as the luxury trains were called — often maintained schedules that equalled or exceeded those of today.

A dining car of the 1930s. Different chairs, different clothes, surely different prices, but the same excitement of a superb dinner while Mid-America slides past your window.

138

# MENUS

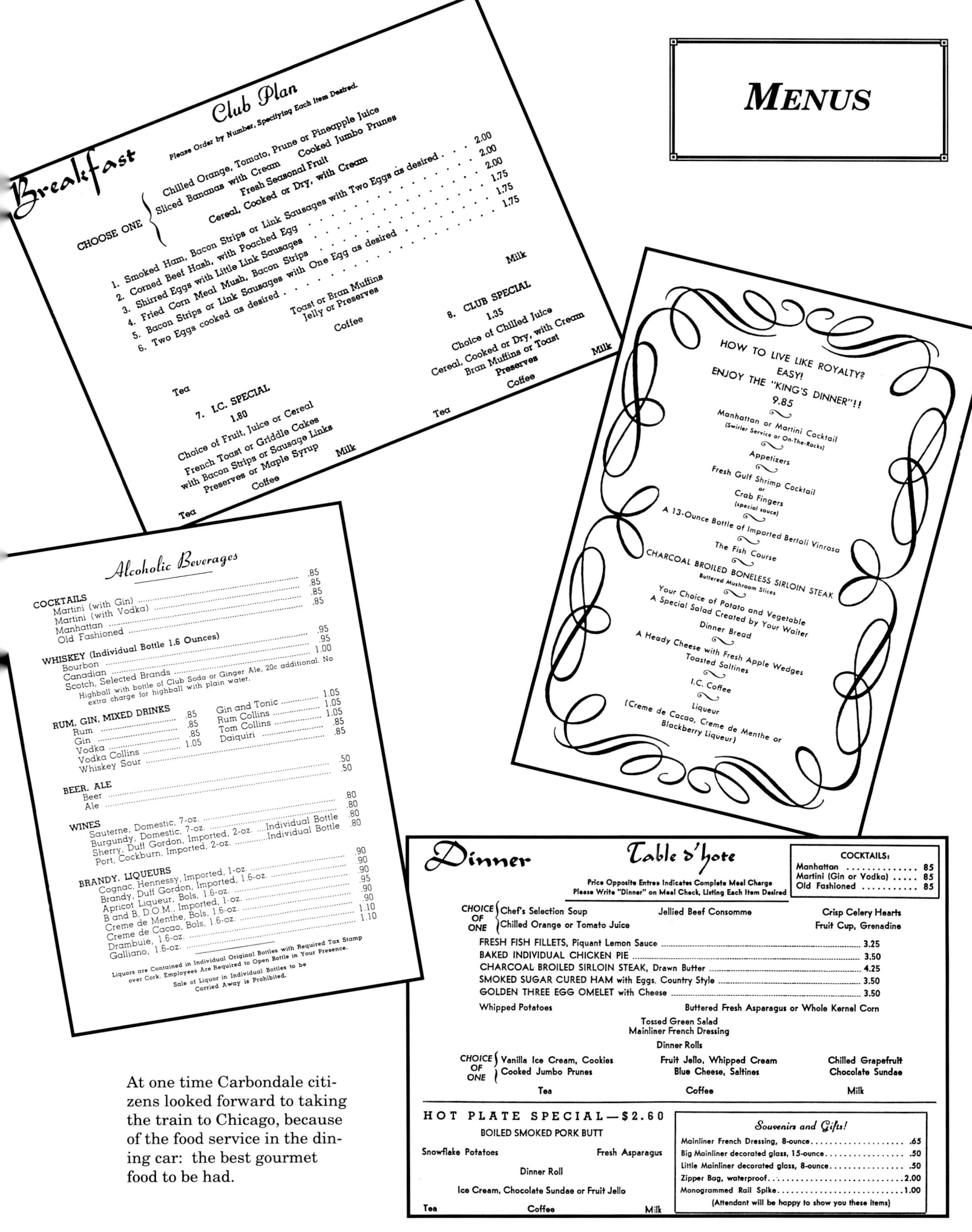

## Breakfast — Club Plan

*Please Order by Number, Specifying Each Item Desired.*

CHOOSE ONE:
- Chilled Orange, Tomato, Prune or Pineapple Juice
- Sliced Bananas with Cream
- Fresh Seasonal Fruit
- Cooked Jumbo Prunes
- Cereal, Cooked or Dry, with Cream

1. Smoked Ham, Bacon Strips or Link Sausages with Two Eggs as desired ........ 2.00
2. Corned Beef Hash, with Poached Egg ........ 2.00
3. Shirred Eggs with Little Link Sausages ........ 2.00
4. Fried Corn Meal Mush, Bacon Strips ........ 1.75
5. Bacon Strips or Link Sausages with One Egg as desired ........ 1.75
6. Two Eggs cooked as desired ........ 1.75

Toast or Bran Muffins
Jelly or Preserves
Coffee    Tea    Milk

7. I.C. SPECIAL — 1.80
Choice of Fruit, Juice or Cereal
French Toast or Griddle Cakes with Bacon Strips or Sausage Links
Preserves or Maple Syrup
Coffee    Tea    Milk

8. CLUB SPECIAL — 1.35
Choice of Chilled Juice
Cereal, Cooked or Dry, with Cream
Bran Muffins or Toast
Preserves
Coffee    Tea    Milk

---

## How to Live Like Royalty? Easy! Enjoy the "King's Dinner"!! — 9.85

Manhattan or Martini Cocktail
*(Swirler Service or On-The-Rocks)*

Appetizers
Fresh Gulf Shrimp Cocktail
or
Crab Fingers
*(special sauce)*

A 13-Ounce Bottle of Imported Bertoli Vinrosa

The Fish Course

CHARCOAL BROILED BONELESS SIRLOIN STEAK
Buttered Mushroom Slices

Your Choice of Potato and Vegetable
A Special Salad Created by Your Waiter
Dinner Bread

A Heady Cheese with Fresh Apple Wedges
Toasted Saltines

I.C. Coffee

Liqueur
*(Creme de Cacao, Creme de Menthe or Blackberry Liqueur)*

---

## Alcoholic Beverages

COCKTAILS
- Martini (with Gin) ........ .85
- Martini (with Vodka) ........ .85
- Manhattan ........ .85
- Old Fashioned ........ .85

WHISKEY (Individual Bottle 1.6 Ounces)
- Bourbon ........ .95
- Canadian ........ .95
- Scotch, Selected Brands ........ 1.00

Highball with bottle of Club Soda or Ginger Ale, 20c additional. No extra charge for highball with plain water.

RUM, GIN, MIXED DRINKS
- Rum ........ .85           Gin and Tonic ........ 1.05
- Gin ........ .85           Rum Collins ........ 1.05
- Vodka ........ .85          Tom Collins ........ 1.05
- Vodka Collins ........ 1.05  Daiquiri ........ .85
- Whiskey Sour ........ .50

BEER, ALE
- Beer ........ .50
- Ale ........ .80

WINES
- Sauterne, Domestic, 7-oz. ........ .80
- Burgundy, Domestic, 7-oz. ........ .80
- Sherry, Duff Gordon, Imported, 2-oz. ........ Individual Bottle .80
- Port, Cockburn, Imported, 2-oz. ........ Individual Bottle .90

BRANDY, LIQUEURS
- Cognac, Hennessy, Imported, 1-oz. ........ .90
- Brandy, Duff Gordon, Imported, 1.6-oz. ........ .90
- Apricot Liqueur, Bols, 1.6-oz. ........ .95
- B and B, D.O.M., Imported, 1-oz. ........ .90
- Creme de Menthe, Bols, 1.6-oz. ........ .90
- Creme de Cacao, Bols, 1.6-oz. ........ 1.10
- Drambuie, 1.6-oz. ........ 1.10
- Galliano, 1.6-oz. ........

Liquors are Contained in Individual Original Bottles with Required Tax Stamp over Cork. Employees Are Required to Open Bottle in Your Presence. Sale of Liquor in Individual Bottles to be Carried Away is Prohibited.

---

At one time Carbondale citizens looked forward to taking the train to Chicago, because of the food service in the dining car: the best gourmet food to be had.

---

## Dinner — Table d'hote

*Price Opposite Entres Indicates Complete Meal Charge*
*Please Write "Dinner" on Meal Check, Listing Each Item Desired*

COCKTAILS:
- Manhattan ........ 85
- Martini (Gin or Vodka) ........ 85
- Old Fashioned ........ 85

CHOICE OF ONE:
- Chef's Selection Soup
- Jellied Beef Consomme
- Crisp Celery Hearts
- Chilled Orange or Tomato Juice
- Fruit Cup, Grenadine

- FRESH FISH FILLETS, Piquant Lemon Sauce ........ 3.25
- BAKED INDIVIDUAL CHICKEN PIE ........ 3.50
- CHARCOAL BROILED SIRLOIN STEAK, Drawn Butter ........ 4.25
- SMOKED SUGAR CURED HAM with Eggs, Country Style ........ 3.50
- GOLDEN THREE EGG OMELET with Cheese ........ 3.50

Whipped Potatoes      Buttered Fresh Asparagus or Whole Kernel Corn

Tossed Green Salad
Mainliner French Dressing

Dinner Rolls

CHOICE OF ONE:
- Vanilla Ice Cream, Cookies
- Cooked Jumbo Prunes
- Fruit Jello, Whipped Cream
- Blue Cheese, Saltines
- Chilled Grapefruit
- Chocolate Sundae

Tea    Coffee    Milk

HOT PLATE SPECIAL — $2.60
BOILED SMOKED PORK BUTT
Snowflake Potatoes      Fresh Asparagus
Dinner Roll
Ice Cream, Chocolate Sundae or Fruit Jello
Tea    Coffee    Milk

### Souvenirs and Gifts!
- Mainliner French Dressing, 8-ounce ........ .65
- Big Mainliner decorated glass, 15-ounce ........ .50
- Little Mainliner decorated glass, 8-ounce ........ .50
- Zipper Bag, waterproof ........ 2.00
- Monogrammed Rail Spike ........ 1.00

*(Attendant will be happy to show you these items)*

139

# Steam Locomotives

The mixed freight train. A staple of the Illinois Central freight business and the cause of countless delays at the various Carbondale grade crossings for more than a hundred years. This kind of mixed freight train is now part of history but the delays are quite current.

An Illinois Central 2-10-2 Central-type locomotive dragging almost a mile of loaded coal cars toward power plants to the North.

Often called "the plumber's nightmare" the back head — the controls — of a steam locomotive was in fact pretty simple. The engineer, in the right-hand seat, controlled the throttle, the locomotive brakes and the train brakes, and the reverse mechanism. Since this locomotive used a mechanical stoker, the fireman in the left-hand seat controlled the shape and intensity of the fire with the valves at the left of the picture. Both carefully watched the array of gauges. But it was the artistry and professionalism of the men who operated these controls that made them the aristocrats of American labor, and made the iron horses behave politely.

The engineer at his post on a steam locomotive. As the engine crew spotted track signals they called out the color or position of the signal to each other so that there could be no mistake about traffic or track conditions ahead.

141

# STEAM LOCOMOTIVES

The Mikado-type was the workhorse of steam locomotives out of the Carbondale roundhouse. The 2-8-2s —locomotive types are named according to their wheel arrangements — were designed for an order from the Government of Japan by the Baldwin Locomotive Company early in the century, and they were named in honor of the Japanese Emperor. During World War II that was considered inappropriate to say the least; so it was ordained that the class be called the MacArthur. Perhaps a few railroad officers complied, but to the operating railroadmen they were still called "Mikes," as they always had been and are to this day.

The larger of the steam switch engine types used in downtown Carbondale. The 0-8-0 type was designed by the United States Railroad Administration during the first World War and served the Nation and its railroads with honor and efficiency until overtaken by the diesel engine mid-century.

This, and countless other Illinois Central passenger trains, was for almost a century the Carbondale's citizen's most important connection to the rest of America and the world.

# Illinois Central

The Illinois Central symbol began as a simple diamond over the words "Illinois Central" to easily identify the company's rolling stock as it was routed to other railroads. The steam locomotives — with one exception — never carried a symbol, only the initials I.C.R.R. on the tender. In time, identifying lettering was added to the simple diamond. The company's first real logo, which early Carbondale citizens will remember, was developed in 1896, with the wording changed in 1923. That symbol was seen in both red and green. The diamond, with variations, returned in 1936 and was seen on the nose of the streamliners and the side of the black freight diesels. In 1966 the so-called "split rail" appeared, showing the profile of a rail which could also be read as IC. Later, after the G. M. & O. merger, the railroad was called Illinois Central Gulf, the split disappeared and the dot was centered and only the letters ICG appeared on the long hood of locomotives. The orange and white color scheme continued with the words on the long hoods of diesel locomotives reflecting the new merged name, Illinois Central Gulf. In 1979 the color scheme was changed to slate gray and burnt orange. After a flurry of management and ownership changes a new mark was adopted. Seen on most of the company's engines today, the new symbol, a black and white device, has no relationship to these historic identifications.

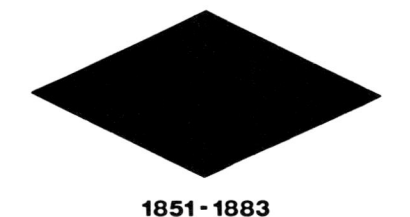

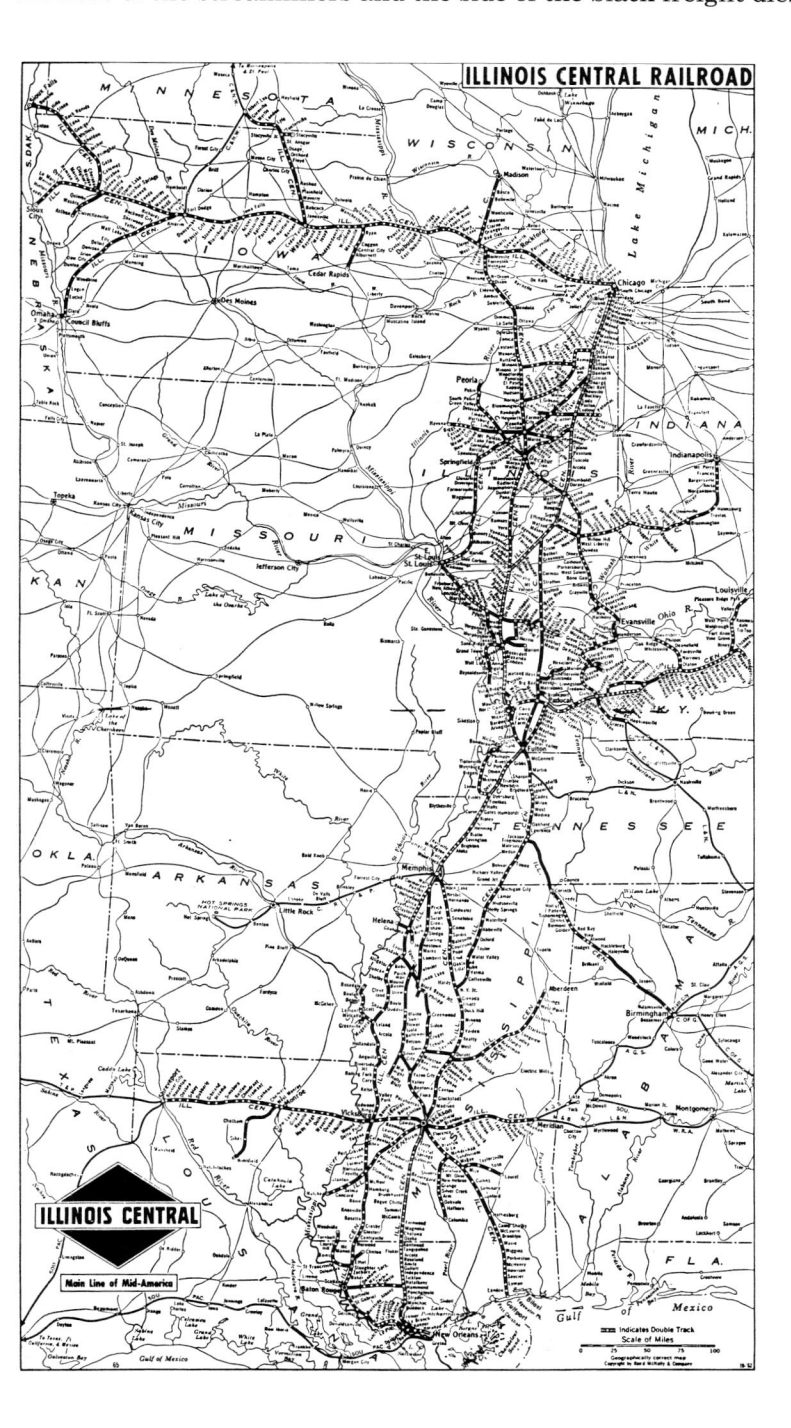

**1851 - 1883**

**1883 - 1896**

**1896 - 1923**

**1923 - 1936**

**1936 - 1950**

**1950 - 1966**

**1966 - 1972**

143

# Division Office

A light dusting of April snow lay on the newly built St. Louis Division headquarters, located in the northeast quarter of the downtown railroad property. The building, along with expanded mechanical facilities, yards, and other improvements resulted from the city's selection as headquarters for the new division.

During the twenties the expanded headquarters building anchored the growing downtown area. The building sat in a park-like area, with mature trees, a gazebo, and working decorative fountain. Alas, only the fountain figure still exists, and is destined for a place of honor in the renovated downtown area.

In 1962, at a typical Illinois Central party to entertain customers are Harry Koonce, Division Superintendant; Harry Williamson, customer; Winton Walkup, Traffic Agent.

The Division Office shortly before it burned to the ground. The downtown economy had slowed to a crawl, the St. Louis Division of the railroad no longer existed, and, perhaps foreshadowing things to come, the park had become a parking lot.

South view of Division office.

145

# Diesels

Although loyalty to some of its largest customers —coal mine owners — caused the I.C. to be among the last national railroad to convert completely to diesel power, the railroad was among the first users of internal combustion in specialized applications. This early diesel helped the railroad reduce smoke along the Chicago lake front.

Bowing to the inevitable, the I. C. began its serious diesel conversion effort during the 1950s, virtually completing it in the 60s. In deference to its traditional coal customers, however, the new locomotives were painted a somber black, unlike the new engines of many railroads that came in all shades of red, yellow, blue, green, and, of all things, purple. While the new equipment was planned to run with a short nose in front, much like a car or truck, experienced engineers, accustomed to a long boiler between them and whatever might be stalled on the track, insisted in running them backwards. The practice still prevails on some railroads, although not on the I. C.

The nose nobody learned to love! The Illinois Central's first diesel streamlined train, *The Green Diamond,* stands for its official portrait in early 1936.

146

Often called by self-styled critics "The Green Worm," the *Diamond* initially ran on the hotly competitive Chicago-Springfield-St.Louis route. As the wartime traffic increased dramatically, the capacity of the little articulated train couldn't be increased, so the *Diamond* was sent to Mississippi where it served on a less heavily travelled run. Later in the war it was retired and stored in the Chicago yards. Badly vandalized, the train was ultimately scrapped and the aluminum found its way into the war effort.

The Illinois Central flagship, The *Panama Limited,* in her new postwar chocolate and orange livery. Initiated in the early days of the twentieth century, and named after the just-completed engineering marvel, the Panama Canal, the *Panama* ran for years behind the company's fastest passenger steam engines and the finest heavyweight passenger equipment available. The locomotive shown, number 4001, was the second such diesel bought for passenger service and the first to carry the name *Panama Limited* on its colorful nose. Despite the fact that the post-war streamliners seemed to herald a bright new day for American passenger service, the fact was that passenger service — and revenue — peaked during the twenties. The depression years of the thirties saw all rail service head into the decline that led, except for special needs of wartime transportation, to the establishment of Amtrak in 1971.

# Diesels

The nose everybody grew to love. The familiar chocolate and orange streamliners that graced Carbondale from the late1930s until a year or so after Amtrak took over the passenger service in 1971. The diamond-shaped logo was still green, since early in the century the official color of the railroad.

The view from the engineer's seat of a modern diesel locomotive. Although the fundamental controls — throttle, brakes and such — remain, the operating techniques needed are quite different. On many locomotives on the rails today computers handle some of the operating details. Still, it's the engineer's artistry that makes it all possible.

Phase two of the Illinois Central streamlining and modernization program, the diesel *City of Miami* locomotive. Electromotive delivered the first of many so-called E6 diesels to the I. C. in 1939. This locomotive, assigned exclusively to the then-new *City of Miami* lightweight train, had more of an automotive than worm-like look and proved to be a spectacular if short-lived sight flashing through Carbondale. It was painted in what the railroad called Fruit Orange with a Tropical Green "bow wave" and roof. The then wife of W. Averell Harriman, a member of the I. C. Board Of Directors at the time, had a good deal to say about the decoration and interiors of this and the earlier *Green Diamond*. After a year or so, more conservative forces saw to it that number 4000 was painted in the more stately chocolate and orange livery that became so familiar to Carbondale observers. Don't spend too much time looking for your grandfather in this photograph. Few pictures of this paint scheme exist and this one, unfortunately, wasn't taken in Carbondale.

148

# KITCHEN

Dinner in the diner, long before the days of Amtrak, was always an exciting experience. Although Pullman porters and dining car employees were not highly paid, these positions were eagerly sought after and commanded considerable respect.

Dining car kitchens from the earliest days were models of efficiency, even if coal-fueled. It wasn't until almost mid-century that an all-electric kitchen appeared on the rails. While such kitchens were in use almost all food was prepared on-board and from fresh ingredients. Today's Amtrak food service owes more to airline food techniques than to the great traditions of the dining cars.

A place for everything and everything in its place. The Pullman kitchen had almost everything you might find in the kitchen of a luxury restaurant except, possibly, room to walk around. In this view of a typical restaurant-on-rails fresh trout are being prepared to order.

149

An aristocrat of American labor. From his seat of honor on the right side of the locomotive, the engineer turns a complicated and ornory beast into a smooth and disciplined source of power. In the days of steam, the typical engineer signed on as a track worker, call boy or telegrapher. His first job aboard the locomotive was as fireman, shovelling tons of coal deftly and precisely into the room-sized firebox during his workday. Only after a long apprenticeship as fireman was he promoted to the grand position of engineer.

Whatever else steam oriented railroad men might think of them, they had to admit that the new diesels were cleaner than the steamers. One member of this crew, shown working the downtown passenger trains, was even able to don a snappy straw hat, unlikely on the old steam switchers.

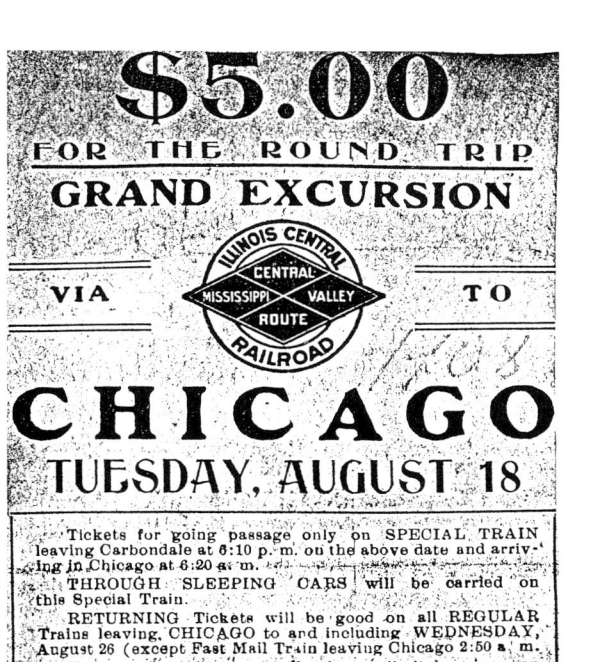

Abraham Lincoln's pass on the Illinois Central railroad. The I. C. was always particularly proud of the men of national importance who helped found, finance, and operate the company over the years. But it was most proud of Lincoln and, to a lessor extent, Stephen A. Douglas. Lincoln was active in the formation of some of the predecessor companies dating from the 1830s, and was General Counsel to the railroad from its founding in 1851 until the day he was nominated for the presidency at Chicago's "Wigwam" convention. While employed by the I. C., Lincoln tried a tax case against various local Illinois governments, then presented to the company the largest attorney-to-client bill on record up to that time, on the order of $5000.00. He ultimately had to go to court himself to collect it.

Above: In 1908, a passenger could take the I.C. from carbondale to Chicago and return for only $5.00.

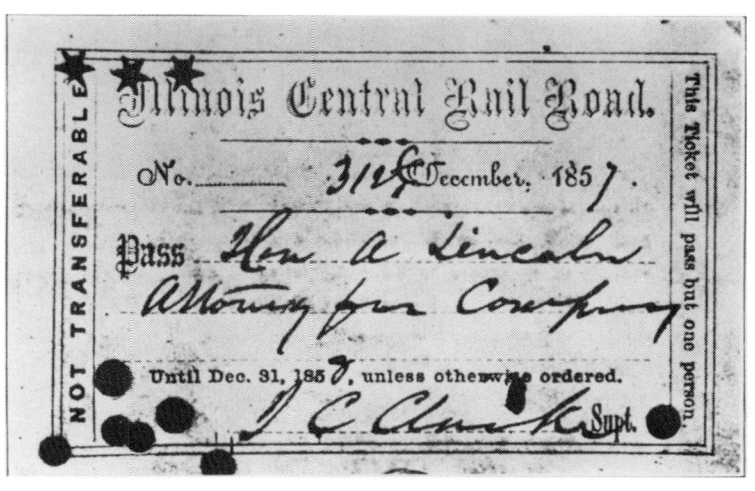

Right: The ticket purchased by the passenger was of two parts: the traveller kept one; the conductor collected the other.

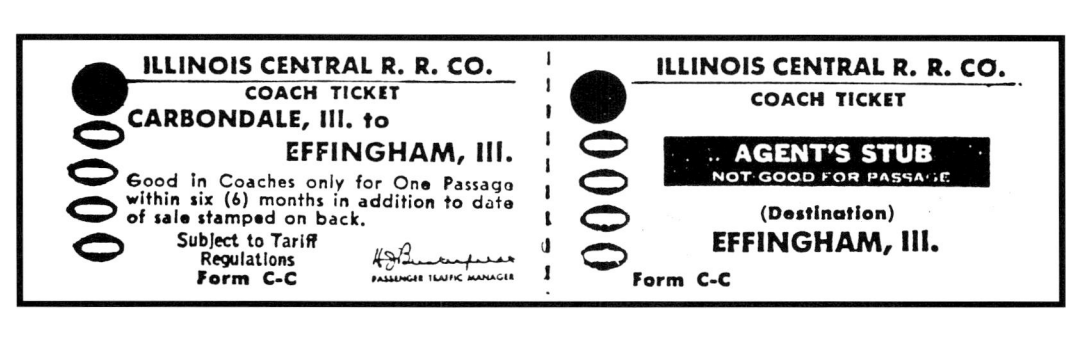

Below: The caboose, once an institution, is now only of the past.

# Roundhouse

Useless relics of the days of steam, these twin coaling towers still stand just north of Carbondale as this is written. The great roundhouse is gone, but these towers, a rusted and immobile turntable and the shop building remain as reminders of the ceaseless activities around a locomotive servicing facility. At the end of its workday the engine was turned over to the service crews, who would drop its ashes, relay the fire, check for damage or wear, fill the tender with coal and water, and have it on the ready-track for the next day's assignment. A major reason for the superiority of diesel power over the steam locomotive was the vast amount of manpower necessary to maintain and operate the steam units. Railroaders like to say that it took ten minutes to find the trouble on an ailing steam locomotive, and three days to fix it. But when a diesel failed it took three days to find the trouble and ten minutes to fix it. When the railroads added up the needed manpower, the diesel won hands down, and the steam engine, at the heart of America's growth and history since 1820, was doomed.

A watercolor of the scene was painted by Paul Lougeay in 1958.

The Carbondale roundhouse during the latter days of steam. The locomotives shown here are both road engines and local switch engines.

The life-blood of a steam locomotive is water, consumed at alarming rates by mile-long freights or fast heavyweight passenger trains. Penstocks such as this one on the I.C. property dotted the railroad, allowing engine crews to refill the tender every hundred miles or so. While the train stood in the station, taking on passengers or waiting for the switch engine to do its work, the fireman would clamor up to the top of the tender, maneuver the spout over the water hatch, and take on thousands of gallons of water in just a few minutes.

# Roundhouse

This yard office stood for many years just north of the roundhouse. The building was demolished in 1988.

The diesel switch engine, the Victor over steam, replaced the steam switcher in railway systems all over the country.

Instead of the traditional gold watch, retiring roundhouse Store Keeper McAnelly (to the right of the range) is presented with a brand new stove at his retirement ceremony in the 1940s. To the right of the guest of honor is roundhouse General Foreman Gene Heisler.

The American Legion, the C.C.H.S. Band, and Carbondale Boy Scout troops present an American flag at a roundhouse ceremony just weeks before the start of World War II. The flagpole stands today in Woodlawn Cemetery on East Main Street.

The Carbondale passenger station on a busy summer afternoon depicts the activity common to that facility.

The freight house, after falling on bad times, originally the point at which all items shipped into Carbondale touched-- shoes to sealing wax to ship models. This building served the community for decades. Whether it stands on the site of the first freight house that Daniel Brush built is a question still under study. In 1991 it is being eyed critically, and its fate is unsettled.

FOURTEENTH SUMMER SESSION
OF THE
## Southern Illinois Normal University
JUNE 17 — JULY 26, 1901
(SIX FULL WEEKS)

Regular work offered by heads of departments. Credits given for completed work.

Reviews in Common Branches and Natural Sciences. Entire equipment of the Institution utilized.

NO TUITION.   INCIDENTAL FEE, ONE DOLLAR.

Persons contemplating attending please send for Syllabus of Work, stating kind desired. Board at reasonable rates.

N. B.
- Spring term opens March 26.
- School Council, April 12 and 13.
- Commencement, June 13.
- Summer Session, June 17 to July 26.

For particulars regarding any features of the Institution, address

D. B. PARKINSON, Carbondale.

The history of Southern Illinois University is treated chronologically in three parts: from 1869 to 1947, from 1948 to 1970, and from 1971 to present. Following this presentation, the growth of the physical plant, and the addition of major buildings, is traced chronologically, beginning with the "old campus," as it existed in the 1930s and 1940s, and then with the development in the 1950s, 1960s, and 1970s, and finally with the dormitories, which are at the end.

# Chapter VI

## Southern Illinois University

The State of Illinois, recognizing the need to train teachers, established Illinois Normal University at Normal, Illinois, in 1857. Many educators and citizens of southern Illinois, thinking that Normal was too far from the southern part of the state and that Normal alone could not provide enough trained teachers for the entire state, pressured for another state normal. In May, 1868, two hundred teachers and superintendents met in Salem, Illinois, to call for a convention with well-defined purposes, one of which was the establishment of a Southern Illinois Normal. A number of communities in the southern part of the state were interested in having a new normal, but on June 24-26, 1868, Carbondale held a meeting which attracted "a thousand leading school men," according to Dean Lentz. He described the meeting: "Carbondale's hospitality to the hundreds of visitors was most cordial; Carbondale homes entertained without charge, and the Illinois Central gave free return transportation to those traveling by rail." Another conference was held in Centralia on September 1-3, 1868, with the main intent to form a Southern Illinois Educational Association. From that meeting a Committee of Fifteen was appointed to encourage the state legislature to approve a normal school to be located in the southern part of the state. On April 20, 1869, the Charter Act was passed by the Illinois General Assembly and signed by Governor John M. Palmer. On August 31, 1869, Carbondale was chosen as the location, reportedly because "Carbondale has never had a drinking saloon, doggery, billiard room or place of dissipation or idle resort within its limits and is absolutely free from these temptations to vice and idleness." In December, 1869, a contract was awarded for the first building, on which Dean Lentz wrote:

*The Trustees awarded a contract in December 1869, for the building and equipment according to the approved plans. The contract was given to James M. Campbell, one of Carbondale's wealthier public-spirited citizens, not on competitive bid, but on Carbondale's guarantee that the building would be completed according to specifications, within a year and at a cost not to exceed $210,00—neither of which conditions was met. Rev. Palmer, a member of the Board, was appointed to superintend construction, and moved to Carbondale to that end. The work of building made rapid progress in the early months of 1870, and the first story of red sandstone, called by a legal fiction the basement, was completed by early May.*

*The ceremony of cornerstone laying, May 17, 1870, was made the occasion for a gala day in Carbondale. Press reporters variously estimated the crowd attracted by the elaborate celebration at ten to twenty thousand people.*

However, the building was not completed until 1874, the result of a number of factors, and the dedication was held on July 1, 1874, when Dr. Robert Allyn was inaugurated president. Classes began on July 2. Prior to that date, on February 26, 1874, the Board of Trustees, which had been appointed by Governor John L. Beveridge in 1873, created the twelve departments, chose the faculty, and adopted the University seal. The twelve departments were Mental Science, Logic, and Teaching; Language and Literature; Mathematics; Natural History; Botany; Physiology; Natural Philosophy and Applied Chemistry; Reading and Elocution; Geography and History; Grammar and Etymology; Vocal Music; Drawing and Writing; Preparatory School; and Model School. Fifty-three students enrolled for the first four-week summer term, mostly consisting of teachers who wanted to qualify for a higher certificate. For the eighteen years of Allyn's headship, he held faculty meetings two or three times a week, but in his philosophy of leadership he considered himself an equal with other members of the faculty. In the fall term of 1874, 143 students were enrolled, but by the end of the year, it had increased to 396.

On November 26, 1883, just about ten years after classes had begun in the Main Building, it burned. E. J. Ingersoll, mayor, called a meeting at the Moody Opera House of the citizens of Carbondale. Contributions of $1,800 were raised that night, and another $5,000 within a week, to construct a temporary building, which Isaac Rapp built in time for occupancy in January. On the day after the fire, the students assembled in the Baptist Church, with, according to Lentz, "A new spirit of loyalty and devotion, a happy augury for a greater Southern. . . ." The rebuilding began in 1885 and was completed and dedicated in 1887, at which time Governor Richard J. Oglesby spoke.

Dr. Allyn retired in 1892 and was succeeded by John Hull, who had been serving as registrar and vice president, but he served only one year. Harvey William Everest, who served as president from 1893 to 1897, put forward a building program, and Altgeld (named for the current governor who supported the program) was dedicated in 1896. For many years this building, which housed at the time the library, and physics, chemistry, and biological science, as well as a big gymnasium, was known as "Old Science."

On Everest's retirement in 1897, Daniel Baldwin Parkinson became president. During his tenure, in 1907, the Illinois General Assembly gave authority to four normal schools to grant a Bachelor of Education degree. Also during his term three additional buildings were completed: Wheeler (in 1904) to house the library, Allyn (1909) to provide a model school, and Anthony Hall (1913) to serve as a dormitory for women as well as a center for social activities of the school. The formal inauguration of Henry William Shryock as president accompanied the dedication of Anthony Hall.

Mr. Shryock served Southern from 1894, when he became head of the English Department, until 1935 when he died in his office in Shryock Auditorium. Dean Lentz writes, "President Shryock had very definite objectives for the advancement of the school's status, but he wisely sought their achievement without fanfare of revolutionary change." Achievements during his tenure included publication of the first *Obelisk*, establishment of a Bureau of Rural School Work (both in 1914), completion of a Power House (1915), building of Shryock Auditorium (dedicated in 1918), publication of the *Egyptian* (1920) as a weekly, completion of the New Gymnasium (now Davies) (1925), and completion of Parkinson Laboratory (1928). In addition, during his term in 1917 the Normal Schools and Teachers Colleges were brought under the authority of the Department of Registration and Education, and a board was established; the first class received degrees in 1922; a Dean of the Faculty was created in 1923 and Dean of Women in 1936; the North Central Association accredited Southern as a degree-conferring teachers college.

When President Shryock died in 1935, Roscoe Pulliam was appointed as the sixth president. During his term of office, the position of Dean of Men was created; he appointed a Council of Administration, consisting of the dean of the faculty, the personnel deans, business manager, registrar, director of teacher training, director of extension, and head of the Education Department. Shortly after a representative of the faculty senate and two from the student council were added. The faculty senate consisted of an elected member from each of the six divisions—social studies, humanities, biological and earth sciences, physical sciences and mathematics, practical arts and crafts, and professional studies—plus one at-large. The student body approved a student council, four from each class, charged with appointment of students on committees, control of student elections, Honors Day and other assemblies, and control of student publications. Such a group was far different from the old plan. Orientation of freshmen gained attention, under the direction of Emma Bowyer, adviser of the freshman class and head of the English Department. One of the most important concerns under Pulliam was the campaign for university status. During his term McAndrew Stadium was completed (1939), and land acquired for the new Training School (Pulliam Hall) in 1940 represented the first expansion of the one-block campus. In 1943 the Crisenberry Bill granted limited University status to Southern. President Pulliam died in 1944.

Chester F. Lay was inaugurated in 1945 and served until 1948. During his tenure in 1947 the Legislature changed the name to Southern Illinois University, and deans of the College of Education, the College of Vocations and Professions, and the College of Liberal Arts and Sciences were named: respectively, Eugene R. Fair, Henry J. Rehn, and Talbert W. Abbott. In addition, the Graduate School, with Willis G. Swartz as chair, granted the first master's degree in Education at the June 1945 commencement to Arthur Madison Smith of Mt. Vernon. Dean Fair was soon replaced by Douglas E. Lawson to head the College of Education. When Chester Lay resigned in 1948, Delyte W. Morris was named eighth president and was formally inaugurated on May 5, 1949, although he began in fall 1948.

In 1948 when Delyte Morris became president of SIU, the campus consisted of approximately one square block; by 1969 it had grown to 7,000 acres. In 1948 760 courses were offered by thirty departments; by 1969 3,400 courses were taught by seventy-four departments. Faculty grew from 181 in 1948 to 942 in 1969, while numbers of student workers increased from 200 in 1948 to 5,500 in 1969. Tax dollars for SIU went from $2,700,134 in 1947 to $112,186,493 in 1969. All of this growth, together with the tremendous growth in the physical plant of the campus, had an extraordinary impact on Carbondale. Although Mill Street was set as a northern boundary and Oakland as a western boundary, the expansion east of the Illinois Central tracks eventually extended to the Pleasant Hill Road on the south, Wall Street on the east, and Freeman Street on the north.

One of Morris' first priorities for SIU was a budget increase, and he enlisted the help of all of Carbondale as well as of the area for a major appropriations bill. In July, 1949, a separate Board of Trustees was approved for SIU, which had previously been governed by the state Teachers College Board. The new training school, Pulliam Hall, was opened in 1949. In 1950 the state Civil Service System was instituted, and Morris asked that US 51 south of town be re-routed. Early in the 1950s the University purchased the houses on the 900 block of University, near Grand, including Carter's Cafe, and those on Grand near University for the first new dormitory since Anthony Hall: Woody Hall, named for Lucy K. Woody, who had been Dean of Women. The University also purchased the area west of Thompson Street, beyond Grand, as well as Thompson Woods and Thompson Lake. In 1953 Woody Hall opened; in 1956 Phase I of Morris Library opened; in 1957 the Agriculture Building and the first phase of Thompson Point were completed; and in 1959 the Home Economics Building (Quigley Hall) was opened. Between 1950 and 1960 enrollment at SIU tripled, from 3,087 to 9,028. In addition to the growth of the physical plant, the University grew in other ways as well. The Vocational Technical Institute opened at Ordill on Crab Orchard Lake, the Press was established, the General Studies Program initiated, the Rehabilitation Institution founded, the outdoor campus at Little Grassy Lake developed, to list a few. During this period also the University established the

Belleville Residence Center and leased Shurtleff College—both steps toward reaching out to the Edwardsville campus.

Between 1960 and 1968 an incredible number of buildings on the campus were built, from dormitories to classroom and laboratory buildings, to those dedicated to other student activities: Dormitories included Greek Row, the second phase of Thompson Point, University Park and Brush Towers, and Evergreen Terrace. Classroom and laboratories included Wham, Lawson, Communications, Technology, Rehn, and Neckers. Others for students were the Student Center, the Arena, and two more phases of the library. In 1967 the SIU basketball team won the NIT. But students in the late 1960s were unhappy, a situation which was reflected in all of Carbondale. They began to protest—against women's hours, vehicle regulations, the academic requirements, housing rules, and they demanded control of the SIU media and rebelled against tuition increases. In May 1969, 2,000 - 2,500

Main I. Although the cornerstone for this, the first building of SIU, was laid on May 17, 1870, the building was not actually completed and dedicated until July 1, 1874. It was approximately 215 by 109 feet, four stories tall, and cost $265,000. On November 26, 1883, it was destroyed by fire.

A temporary frame building, occupied on January 24, 1887.

Above: The temporary building, with power plant.

Right: Lake Ridgeway (south of Davies Gymnasium and northeast of Anthony Hall) was a small body of water originally used in the construction of the first Main building. Before it was filled in so that the area could be used for a parking lot, the students often used it as a dunking pool.

students held a sit-in on Morris' lawn on the campus, and on June 8, 1969, Old Main was burned. In September of that year Morris was heavily criticized for building University House (Stone House), although the Board of Trustees had given approval. In November Clement Stone contributed one million dollars to cover the cost of the house. In June 1970 Morris gave up the presidency. Enrollment had climbed to 22,625 in 1970 on the Carbondale campus, with a total of 35,154 on both campuses.

Between 1970 and 1980, SIU had a series of presidents: Robert G. Layer in 1971-72, David R. Derge in 1972-74, Hiram H. Lesar in 1974, as an interim, followed by Warren W. Brandt from 1974 to 1979. In 1980 Albert Somit became president until 1986, and was followed by John C. Guyon, the current president. In the early 1970s instruction in both medicine and law rounded out the academic offerings. SIU had indeed become the major industry in Carbondale.

A view of Paul and Virginia and the area looking east, in 1887.

Paul and Virginia, the statue of two children, has stood in the fountain just east of Old Main since 1887. It was a gift from the class of 1887 and was given one hundred years after the publication of "Paul et Virginie" by a French poet. The President's Council of the SIU Foundation uses the statue as a symbol which represents Southern Illinois University.

Main II, commonly known as "Old Main," was rededicated on February 24, 1887.

The first president, Robert Allyn, served from 1874 to 1892. Previously he had been president of McKendree College at Lebanon.

John Hull served as president from 1892 to 1893. He resigned to become president of the State Normal School at River Falls, Wisconsin.

Harvey William Everest was president from 1893 to 1897, coming to SINU from Garfield University (Wichita, Kansas) where he had been president.

Daniel Baldwin Parkinson was president from 1897 to 1913, during which Southern began expansion, of both the academic program and the physical plant.

Henry William Shryock, fifth president, from 1913 to 1935, when the auditorium and the gymnasium and the science building were built. Mr. Shryock died in his office of a heart attack, after forty-one years of service to Southern, nineteen as an English teacher and twenty-two as president. He left a fully accredited Teachers College.

Roscoe Pulliam, president from 1935 to 1944. During his tenure a major step led toward democracy within the school, with the creation of a faculty senate and a student council of representatives from the four classes. The first steps were taken toward a pre-registration system and orientation program for freshmen. But the major accomplishment during his time was the granting of University status in 1943.

Chester F. Lay, president from 1945 to 1948. While Lay was president, the Graduate School was developed under Dean Willis Swartz, and the undergraduate colleges were organized: Education, Dean Eugene R. Fair; Liberal Arts and Sciences, Dean T. W. Abbott; and Vocational and Professions, Dean Henry J. Rehn.

President Parkinson's office in Old Main, on the second floor.

The front entrance of the campus (corner of Grand and University).

163

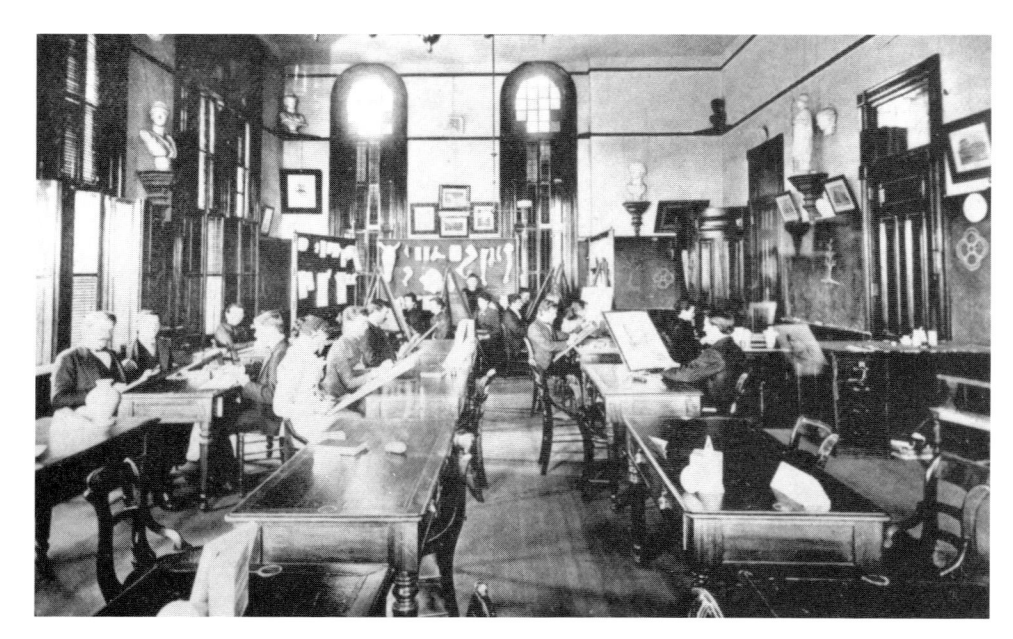

The Art Room in Old Main in the 1890s. This picture originally appeared in the 1894-95 SINU Catalog.

A manual training class in 1910, in Old Main.

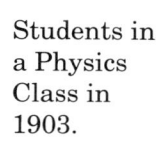

Students in a Physics Class in 1903.

A co-ed physical education class in the "Old Gym" in Altgeld in 1903.

A student assembly in Normal Hall in Old Main, 1908. The same area was used as a study hall, at which time women sat on one side and men on the other.

An 1890s class in physical training, the Model School class.

The 1914 SINU football team: 1 Hamilton, 2 Kilgore, 3 Finn, 4 Kelly, 5 Smith, 6 C. Hays, 7 Bass, 8 Marshall, 9 E. Parker, 10 E. Harris, 11 Etherton, 12 O. Boswell, 13      , 14 Lee, 15 Allen, 16 F. Hays, 17 Snyder, 18 Dodge, 19 Gains, 20 Warren, 21 Shoemaker, 22 J. Harris, 23 Roberts, 24 P. Smith, 25 Vick, 26 McAndrew (coach), 27 Feller.

The women's basketball team in 1906.

In 1904 basketball practice was done outside.

The men's basketball team in 1905.

The Douglas Corps Cadets, the result of a military department, authorized by the board in 1878. Members were male students who were not required, but expected, to participate. The War Department of the federal government supplied equipment and West Point graduates as instructors. The program ended in 1889 and was replaced by "physical culture."

The SINU Men's Glee Club, directed by Professor George W. Smith (Head of the History Department), first appeared at the dedication of Old Science (Altgeld) in the fall of 1896. Bottom, left to right: Dell Lee, Harry J. Alvis, H. L. Freeland, H. W. Temple, Walter E. Stewart, George W. Smith; top, W. G. Cisne, A. H. Burton, W. Gordon Murphy, Chester Arthur Lee, Simeon E. Boomer, T. B. F. Smith, A. Z. Rice, J. Oscar Marberry.

The class of 1899: Bottom, left to right: Etherton, Harris, Pruett, Karraker, Marchildon, Webkemeyer; middle, Stewart, Cisne, Murphey, Grove, Brewster, Roe, Palmer, Brainard, Blake; top, Hooker, Crawford, Haldaman, McKittrick, Brainard, McConaghie.

The Junior Class in 1908: Bottom, left to right: Estelle Hooker, Ethel Maddoz, Ina Metz, Helen Winters, Eunice Taylor, Julia Mitchell, Hallie Winchester; second, ? , Edith Palmer, Carrie —-, W. Hudgen, Clara Barton, Elloise Sheppard, Nina Shelton, ? , Annie Hayden, —- Allen, Gertrude DeGelder; third, Nellie Bouchier, Lipe, Ruth McCreery, ? , ? , Jennie Mitchell, Margaret Porter, Daisy Angell, Velma Harris, Effie Risby, Anna New; fourth, T. H. Shuette, Fred Brown, Ezra Latham, ? , Walter Merryman, ? ; fifth, Chester Hawford, Marion Coker, Ward Cotter, Glenn Brown.

Graduation, in 1908, was held on the campus, with trees as surroundings.

Graduation, 1909. The speaker was William Jennings Bryan, obviously a big attraction which drew many people to the campus.

169

Tennis in the 1930s was on a court east of Davies Gymnasium and Wheeler (where U.S. 51 is in 1991).

A baseball game on the new athletic field of SINU in the 1930s.

The 1928 women's senior basketball team: first row, Jewel Truelove, Mary Matthes, Emma Jean Wiggs, Margaret Armentrout, Juanita Benger; back, Ruby Kenley, —- Stephens, Mable Cope.

Students in the first floor reading room of Wheeler Library in the 1930s.

The Zetetic Literary Society in 1936, Dean Wham lecturing. This group, organized in 1874 and the oldest organization on the campus, was the counterpart of the Socratic Society. Both featured speakers on current events and literary works, and in their early days, presented a variety of programs for the entertainment of the university community.

The 1932 May Fete, presented annually by the Women's Physical Education Department. The *Obelisk* of 1932 describes it as a program composed of dances. A May Queen was elected and presented at this occasion. Lillian Hudspeth was the crown bearer in the picture.

The interior of the Old Cafeteria, probably in the 1940s.

The exterior of the Cafeteria, which was on the corner of Thompson and Chautauqua. (Faner Hall now stands on the site.)

Trobaugh's Store in the end of one of the barracks on Thompson Street.

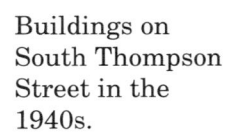

Buildings on South Thompson Street in the 1940s.

Doing their laundry in the basement of Johnson's Coop are Dorothy Paine (Benton), Jo Beth Goforth (Pinckneyville), and Gwyneth Williams (Christopher). ca. 1940s.

Broadcasting a 1947 basketball game in the (Davies) gym are Jim Bolen, Don Boudreau and Paul McRoy (WCIL owner).

Benny Goodman, who came to campus for the 1948 Springfest, joins local musicians at the Spinning Wheel: left to right, Tommy Lawson, Gene Stiman (who later joined the Goodman Band), Jim Bolen, Walt Stocks; seated, Floyd Mooreland, Jimmy Johns.

# HOMECOMING QUEENS

SINU Queen in 1926: Lydia Davis.

SINU Queen in 1930: Alice Hill Crowell.

SINU Queen in 1936: Betty Vick.

SIU Queen in 1955: Marilyn Liebig.

# UNIVERSITY SCHOOL

The Model School, or Training School, from the beginning of SIU history, was an important part of the institution. Shown in front of Allyn are first graders in 1914: first row, Clyde Crayhay, Jim Wilier, Hal Hall, Elma Spiller, Bessie Smith, Elliott Pearce, Gladys Norton, Earl Hanson, Frances Laudon; second, Wesley Baker, Trissie Hughes, G. Biggs, Margaret Gunn, Dorothy Furr, Ellen Bryden, Stewart Williams, Charles Goodall, ? , George Harris.

In 1907, children in a University School handicraft class.

University School students leave for a class trip in 1939. Principal at that time was Hal Hall.

175

President Delyte W. Morris, at his desk in the inner President's office in Shryock Auditorium, in 1948. He served as president from 1948 to 1970, during which SIU grew into a major university in the nation. In 1949 the first Board of Trustees was appointed; in 1959 the first doctorate was awarded; in 1963 legislative restrictions were removed, and in 1969 the School of Law and the School of Medicine were approved. During Morris' tenure the key word was innovation, in all facets of the university.

On May 5, 1949, following the inaugural ceremonies, was a reception in Anthony Hall. In the receiving line, left to right, are Dr. Leo J. Brown (president of the Alumni Association); Mrs. Delyte Morris; President Morris; Mrs. Robert W. Davis, shaking hands with Lucy K. Woody (Dean of Women); Colonel Robert W. Davis (member of the Teachers College Board), and Professor T.W. Abbott (Dean of the College of Liberal Arts and Sciences).

In 1951, after Pulliam Hall was opened, housing the training school, an open house was held on November 16. Shown here are Nancy Pearce, third grader, showing her desk to President Morris and Governor Adlai E. Stevenson.

The Air Force ROTC had come to Southern by 1952; here the cadets parade for a reviewing party in McAndrew Stadium. (Note the field and the surrounding area in the background. To the left is the old power plant.)

In 1949 a University Council served as advisers to the president: left to right are Harold E. Briggs, W. C. McDaniel, Robert H. Mueller, W. B. Schneider, I. Clark Davis, Ted R. Ragsdale, Lewis A. Maverick, Burnett H. Shryock, Willis E. Malone, C. Horton Talley, Hilda A. Stein, Donald A. Ingli, Marshall S. Hiskey, Charles D. Tenney, and Delyte W. Morris.

President and Mrs. Morris constantly entertained the university community. Shown here is a typical scene at the president's home, on November 24, 1952; after a dinner for the Cross Country team, three members relax: Dick Gregory, Gene Haile, and Danny Smith.

Every Thursday at 10:00 was mandatory convocation (earlier called Chapel) in Shryock Auditorium. President Morris is addressing the freshman class in September, 1954.

Another typical scene was the annual watermelon feast for freshmen, held at the president's house until it was outgrown. This one was in 1954.

On August 22, 1955, the 5,000th student registered for fall term: Imogene Dodillet. Watching President Morris shake hands with another student is Robert A. McGrath, Registrar.

An annual event was the Alpha Phi Omega overnight trail ride. The group is relaxing at the end of the day.

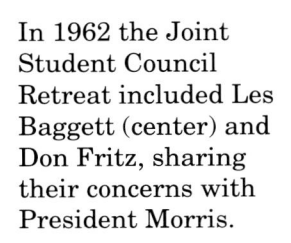

In 1962 the Joint Student Council Retreat included Les Baggett (center) and Don Fritz, sharing their concerns with President Morris.

179

The Christmas holidays were a special time in Morris' tenure. Here in 1953 carolers are being served punch: Esther Andres, Farris McCadney, Dorothy Waltemate, and Delores Armstrong.

The Madrigal Singers at the president's house during Christmas Week, 1953.

The Madrigals sing at Christmas Assembly in 1954.

Jim Hart played football at SIU in 1963-65, and then became a member of the St. Louis Cardinal football team. He returned to SIU in 1988 to become Athletic Director.

The Sigma Pi winning float in the 1953 Homecoming Parade, shown on South Illinois Avenue, between the Varsity Theater and the Bus Depot.

At Homecoming 1956, Mr. Vandeveer presented Salukis Burydown Datis and Ornah Parouk at halftime. Looking on are, left to right, Robert Odaniell, Mr. Vandeveer, R. K. Dillinger, Sandra Unger, President Morris, and Guy W. Lambert.

181

At the cornerstone laying for Morris Library, June 11, 1955, are Governor William G. Stratton and Charles Carpentier (Secretary of State) with President Morris. During each of the eight years that Stratton was governor, he dedicated a building on the SIU campus.

On May 5, 1954, Eleanor Roosevelt was a guest on campus. Shaking hands with her at a reception in the president's home was George H. Hand (Vice President for Business Affairs at SIU). Behind him is his son, Randolph Hand.

On June 6, 1953, SIU celebrated Alumni Day and laid the cornerstones for two buildings: Life Science (I) and Woody Hall. The platform party shown here is at Woody Hall.

Richard M. Nixon (Vice President of the United States) and the official party pass in review of the SIU honor guard on the campus.

At a reception honoring graduates and their parents following graduation on June 15, 1958, is the receiving line, left to right, Dale Cozad (president of the 1958 class), Mrs. Stratton, Governor Stratton, President Morris, and John S. Rendleman (Assistant to the President). The reception was in the Morris' backyard.

In the same backyard, on September 30, 1958, the University Women's Club held their annual style show.

Certainly one of the saddest days in the history of SIU was June 8, 1969, when Old Main was burned.

But a happy occasion in 1972 was the dedication of Martin Baseball Field. Left to right, Bill Freeburg, Paul Restivo, Larry Shockey, Glen "Abe" Martin, John Stotlar, Bill Bleyer, Roger Spear, Bill O'Brien, and Bob Odaniell.

An innovation on the SIU campus was the Cardboard Boat Regatta (begun by Richard Archer in 1974). For many years this event was a part of Spring Festival, but recently it has been held on a separate weekend. This photo, taken in 1987, shows the Vogue Award winner; that year 160 boats competed before 15,000 spectators.

The Marching Salukis, under the direction of Don Cannedy in 1961, began to include jazz in their selections and changed from traditional band uniforms to the tuxedo look. At that time, some of the band were in traditional tuxedos, some in red plaid, and some in red tuxedo jackets, topped by a black homberg. Michael Hanes followed Cannedy in 1965, and continued the look. Later the colors changed to Saluki colors of maroon and white. Keeping the tuxedo look, they went to ruffled shirts and maroon tuxedo; then in 1990 they changed to white dinner jackets with maroon pants and vests. Some of the band are pictured here in 1984 with Governor James Thompson.

The Campus Lake offers a variety of recreational facilities: a boat dock, fishing, and a beach. This group was enjoying the beach on Memorial Day in 1964.

Buckminster Fuller came to SIU as part of the Visiting Scholars Program and stayed for a long period. His influence is reflected in this photograph of students moving a geodesic dome from Greek Row to the Spring Festival Midway, in 1963.

Co-Captians Ralph Johnson and Walt Frazier with the coveted NIT trophy in 1967. Frazier was named Most Valuable Player in the tournament. That game was the last college basketball game played in Madison Square Gardens.

The Madison Square Garden (NY) sign tells it all, except the date, which was 1967.

# SALUKI SPORTS

Fans at the game with the Saluki mascot.

The 1966-67 Saluki Basketball Team, which won the NIT.

186

David Lee, a 400-meter intermediate hurdler, set the school record in 1980, which still stands, of 48.87 seconds. He competed in the Moscow Olympics in 1980. He won thirteen individual first places in Missouri Valley Conference championship meets.

Charlie Vaughn, from Tamms, Il., was recruited by SIU basketball coach Harry Gallatin. In his career at SIU, 1959 through 1962, he set the University all-team scoring record (2,088 points), and the season scoring record (779 points in 1960).

Left to right are Parry Duncan, Tony Adams, ESPN announcer, Elvis Forde and Michael Franks, who had just set a new American collegiate record in the mile relay (3:00.78 minutes) in 1984. This team won the mile relay at the Kansas, Texas, and Drake relays.

The key play in the 1983 National football Championship NCAA I-AA at Charleston, South Carolina. SIU led by 10-0, but this play, with Quarterback Rick Johnson scoring on a one-yard quarterback sneak, midway in the third quarter, gave SIU a 17-0 lead. The Salukis, coached by Rey Dempsey, won the game over Western Carolina by 43-7.

One of the early projects of the University Press was the publication of The London Stage. This photograph in 1959 shows President Morris signing the agreements to publish. Seated, left to right: Charles D. Tenney (Vice President for Instruction); Morris; Vernon Sternberg (Director of the University Press). Standing, left to right: John S. Rendleman (Legal Counsel); Willis G. Swartz, Dean of the Graduate School; John O. Anderson (Assistant Dean in Charge of Research).

The Class of 1913 has celebrated many reunions. Shown here at Giant City Lodge in 1951, celebrating the 38th reunion, are: first row, left to right, Mrs. Karl Kraatz, Mrs. Glenn O. Brown, Mrs. Guy A. Gladson, Mrs. Clyde M. Brooks, Mrs. Albert Eads, and Mrs. Ted R. Ragsdale; kneeling, Carney Chapman, Mrs. Guy Karraker, Mary Entsminger, Mrs. Wallace Karraker; third row, Dr. Clyde M. Brooks, Leland P. Lingle, Glenn O. Brown, Guy W. Karraker, Lowell E. Roberts, Mrs. D. W. Morris, Mrs. Robert Browne, Mrs. W. W. Vandeveer, Dr. Percival Bailey, Karl Kraatz; fourth row, Paul Furr, Ted R. Ragsdale, Guy A. Gladson, W. W. Vandeveer, Robert Browne, D. W. Morris, Leland P. Lingle, and Albert Eads.

The 85th Commencement, on June 15, 1960, was held in McAndrew Stadium. (Commencement had long since outgrown Shryock Auditorium—the last scheduled exercise held there was in 1949). Afterwards, the program moved to the Arena, and in recent years, it has been divided into separate exercises for the undergraduate colleges, with the graduate program in the Arena.

In 1971-72 the Administrative Council of the University: seated, left to right: Robert G. Layer (Chancellor of the Carbondale Campus—note that the titles have been reversed); Clarence W. Stephens, Chair of the Council; John S. Rendleman (Chancellor of the Edwardsville Campus). Standing: Ralph W. Ruffner (System Vice President), James M. Brown (chief of the Board staff), and Isaac P. Brackett (System Vice President).

David R. Derge, President of SIU, 1972-74.

Right: Warren Brandt, President 1974-79.

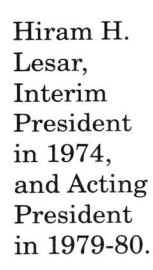

Hiram H. Lesar, Interim President in 1974, and Acting President in 1979-80.

Albert Somit, President 1980-87.

John Guyon, President 1987—.

189

# OLD CAMPUS

Main II, as it appeared in early days, was the center of the campus. It was called Old main throughout most of its history.

Altgeld, known to some generations of SIU students as Old Science, was built in 1896 to house the science departments and the gymnasium, but currently serves the School of Music. (It was named for Governor John Altgeld—1883-1897.)

Wheeler, the third major campus building, was built in 1904 and served as the library until 1956. (It was named for Judge Samuel P. Wheeler, an early member and president of the Board of Trustees, 1885-1893).

Shryock Auditorium, completed and opened on April 4, 1918, when William Howard Taft, former U.S. President, gave the first lecture. Named for Henry W. Shryock, the fifth president of SIU, the building was renovated in 1971. It has been the location for mandatory chapel, freshman convocation, and countless performances by students and professionals.

Left: Built in 1908, the Allyn Building, named for Robert Allyn, the first president of SIU, was designed for and used by the training school, both grade and high school classes, until Pulliam Hall was completed. It now houses the School of Art. The Vergette Gallery, located in this building, is named for Nicholas Vergette, an internationally known sculptor who was Professor of Art, 1959-1974.

Above: Parkinson Laboratory, built in 1928 and named for Daniel B. Parkinson, originally housed chemistry, physics, industrial arts, and the bookstore. Currently it is used by Geology. Browne Auditorium, added in 1959 as a chemistry auditorium, is named for George M. Browne, Professor of Physical and Chemical Sciences, 1903-1936.

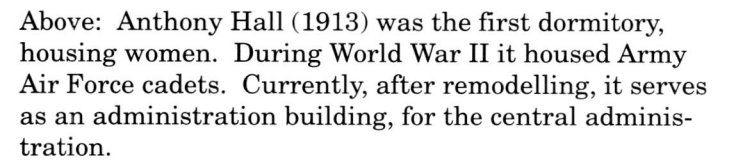

Above: Anthony Hall (1913) was the first dormitory, housing women. During World War II it housed Army Air Force cadets. Currently, after remodelling, it serves as an administration building, for the central administration.

Right: The "new gym" built in 1925 replaced the old gymnasium in Altgeld Hall. It housed both men's and women's physical education departments until the Arena was built. Currently it houses physical education (the separation no longer exists). It is named for Dorothy R. Davies, chair of women's physical education from 1939-1974.

Originally called the Home Economics Building when it was built in 1959, this building is known as Quigley, named for Eileen E. Quigley, Professor, Chair, and Dean of the School of Home Economics from 1948 to 1969. In 1973 this unit became part of the College of Human Resources.

The Agriculture Building, completed in 1957, houses the School of Agriculture, and contains Muckelroy Auditorium, named for Renzo Muckelroy, Professor of Agriculture and Chair, 1911-1945.

Morris Library, named for Delyte Morris, has been built in stages; the original was dedicated in 1958, although construction began in 1955. It houses one of the largest open-stack collections in the United States.

Pulliam Hall, known as University School until 1965, was completed in its first stage in 1951 and the second stage in 1954. It is named for Roscoe Pulliam, sixth president, and houses Furr Auditorium, named for William A. Furr, and Cisne Hall, named for Willis Cisne. It has undergone extensive remodelling in 1989-91 and no longer houses the training school, for which it was originally built, because the University gave up an on-campus training school.

Above: The Hiram H. Lesar Law Building opened in 1982 and houses the Law School. It is named for the first dean of the School of Law.

Below: The Communications Building, a complex for the School of Journalism, the Departments of Speech Communications, Communication Disorders and Sciences, Cinema and Photography, Radio-Television, Theater, and the Broadcasting Services (WSIU-FM and WSIU-TV), was built in 1966. It also houses McLeod Playhouse, named for Archibald McLeod, former chair of Theater and the Marion Kleinau Theater. It serves the *Daily Egyptian* staff as well.

Below: Lawson Hall, built in 1965, is an unusual building, with many pie-shaped lecture rooms. It is named for Douglas E. Lawson, Professor of Education and Dean of the College of Education, 1935-1961.

Above: Faner Hall. An immense structure (three blocks long) was originally planned as a Humanities Building. A reinforced concrete construction costing $13 million, it was completed in 1975. Since planning for this building was in progress when Old Main was burned in 1969, a third wing, "C" wing, was added to the plans to give additional space on the campus. It is named for Robert Dunn Faner, Professor of English from 1930 to 1967 and Chair of the Department of English from 1963 to 1967. It houses primarily the College of Liberal Arts, the University Museum, Institutional Research, and the Department of Computer Science and its laboratories.

The W. Clement and Jessie V. Stone House, originally known as University House, was completed in the spring of 1971. It is named for the Stones, who contributed substantially to the financing. It serves as the setting for many official activities.

The Student Recreation Center was built in 1977, at a cost of $9.6 million, paid by student fees. It houses gymnasiums, an olympic-sized pool, handball and racquetball courts, exercise and weight-training rooms, and indoor track and tennis courts. The second stage was completed in 1990.

The Arena contains the largest indoor seating capacity on the campus, 10,014 for basketball games and 4,500 to 11,000 for concert and lecture programs. It was built in 1964 and includes an office and classroom wing, Lingle Hall, named for Leland P. Lingle, track and field coach, 1927-1960.

The Student Center, originally built in 1961 and added on to until 1971, houses the University Bookstore, offices, study lounges, meeting rooms, recreational facilities, an auditorium, restaurants and cafeterias, ballrooms, video lounges, and craft shops.

# DORMITORIES

One of the three 17-story buildings in Brush Towers, shown in 1965 on the dedication day. The University Park and Brush Towers housing area east of the Illinois Central tracks was developed in two stages, in 1965 and 1968.

The three towers are named for English Department faculty: W.B. Schneider, Julia Neely, and Mae T. Smith.

Woody Hall, built in 1953 as a women's dormitory, was named for Lucy K. Woody, a member of the faculty from 1911 to 1949. She was Professor of Home Economics, Chair of Household Arts, and from 1926 Dean of Women. In 1968 it ceased being a dormitory and currently houses a number of offices: Admissions and Records, Student Work and Financial Assistance, the Graduate School, Pre-Major Advisement, and other offices.

The Thompson Point dormitories (dedicated in 1957) and Greek Row (built in 1960-62) are located on Campus Lake. Thompson Point contains twelve buildings and Greek Row fifteen.

# ACKNOWLEDGEMENTS

The photographs in this book come from individuals and collections, both of which are essential to the purpose. For their major collections, I thank Jean Smith Foley, Elizabeth Lutz Archer, Monte and Bud Stotlar, Polly Winkler Mitchell, Helen Sorgen Deniston, Tom and Tim Langdon, Dorothy Morris, Mabel Schwartz, and Bill Etherton, who graciously sent the collection of his mother, Julia Mitchell Etherton. For almost the entire chapter of the Illinois Centrail Railroad I am indebted to Bill Schremp, who provided not only pictures but expertise as well as captions. To many people, too numerous to list here, whom I called for help and information, I am grateful. But especially among these are Mary and Leo Brown, Rosetta O'Neal, Joan Foley Martin, and Mary Curd Simon, who consented to critique the manuscript.

Bernie Weithorn of Photographic Services, Jack Dyer of University Relations, Terry Svec and Joel Maring of PhotoCommunications, and Pete Brown of University News Service were all outstanding in their efforts to help. The works of Susan Maycock, John W. D. Wright, and Eli Lentz were extremely valuable in providing information.

Also I thank Earline Elkins, Theresa Rust, and the First National Bank and Trust.

Brad Baraks was, of course, essential.

My daughter, Sarah Merideth, was indispensable: she put all of the copy onto the computer and helped in the editing and proofing. And I thank my husband, Ellis, who answered many questions, and my family, who put up with me all summer.

# CONTRIBUTORS

Elizabeth Lutz Archer
Judy Baine
Jean and Troy Barrett
Jim Bolen
Linda Brandon
Leo and Mary Brown
Carbondale City Clerk's Office
Carbondale Park District & George Whitehead
Carbondale Uptown Inc.
Sue Casebeer
Dorothy Chaney
John Cherry
Gene Paul Crawshaw
Clark Davis & Bank of Carbondale
George and Helen Deniston
James Dickey
Judy Heisler Dillinger
Randy Dominick
Paul Dvorshock
Mary Elston
Bill Etherton
Jean Smith Foley
John L. Golliher
Chester Hager
Taffie Helleny
Steve Higgerson

Fred Huff
Joan and William N. Huffman
Larry Jacober & Elementary School District
Richard Kelley
David Kenney
Lyndall Kiefer
Mary Alice Kimmel
Jerry Kloever
Harry Koonce
Tom and Tim Langdon
Elizabeth Lewis
Melvin Lipe & Landmark Bank
Paul Lougeay
George Maroney & Memorial Hospital
Joan Foley Martin
Marlene Matten
Trish Medlin
A.B. Mifflin
Everett and Alberta Miller
Dorothy A. Mills
Ellis L. Mitchell
Polly Winkler Mitchell
Tom Mofield
Elizabeth Mitchell Montgomery
Dorothy Morris
Emilyn and James Morris

Rosetta O'Neal
Barbara and Gary Parrish
Naomi Patheal and First Christian Church
Gwen Peyton
Frances Phillips
Duane Pick
Dorcy Prosser
Frances Dillinger Reid
Jane and Charles Renfro
Bill Schremp
Mabel Schwartz
Mary Curd Simon
Staff, Carbondale Public Library
Staff, First Baptist Church
Staff, First Methodist Church
Staff, First Presbyterian Church
Staff, University Baptist Church
Staff, Walnut Street Baptist Church
Monte and John Stotler
Orpha Striegel
Jim Temple
E.W. Vogler
Bernie Weithorn
Wayne and Deanna Wheeles
Mary McRoy White
John Wright

# BIBLIOGRAPHY

Allen, John W.O. *Jackson County Notes.* Carbondale, IL: Southern Illinois Normal University, 1945.

Allen, John W.O. *Legends and Lore of Southern Illinois.* Carbondale, IL: University Graphics, 1963.

Alumni Association. *Southern Illinois Normal University Alumnae Directory.* Carbondale, IL: 1945.

Alumni Association. *Quarter Centennial Anniversary Souvenir of the Southern Illinois State Normal University.* Carbondale, IL: Carbondale Free Press, 1899.

Bond, Stanton. *1970 Carbondale Annual Report.* Carbondale, IL: Ace Advertising Design, 1971.

Brown, Leo J. *The Carbondale Clinic: The First 50 Years.* Privately printed, 1988.

Brown, Mary Barrow. *Growing up in Carbondale, Illinois.* Privately printed, 1986.

Carbondale Chamber of Commerce. *Capsule History of Carbondale's First 100 Years.* Unpublished, 1952.

Brush, Daniel Harmon. *Growing Up with Southen Illinois, 1820-1861.* Chicago: R. R. Donnelley and Sons Co., 1944.

Dorsey, May. *Through the Years 1861-1980.* Privately printed, 1981.

Jackson County Historical Society. *History of Jackson County, Illinois.* Philadelphia: Brink, McDonough Company, 1878.

Lentz, Eli G. Southern Illinois University: *The First Seventy-Five Years, 1874-1949.* Carbondale, IL: Diamond Jubilee Committee, 1949.

Lentz, Eli G. and R. L. Dillinger. *History of Shekinah Lodge #241, 1857-1957.* Carbondale, IL: Dunaway-Sinclair Inc. Printing.

Lentz, Eli G. *Seventy Five Years in Retrospect.* Carbondale, IL: University Editorial Board, Charles D. Tenney, Chairman, 1955.

Maycock, Susan E. *An Architectural History of Carbondale, Illinois.* Carbondale, IL: Southern Illinois Univerity Press, 1983.

Mitchell, Betty. *Delyte Morris of Southern Illinois University.* Carbondale, IL: Southern Illinois University Press, 1988.

Morris, Emilyn. *Miss Lillian's Town, Carbondale, Illinois, 1823-1973.* Privately printed, 1980.

Neely, Aileen. *Days of Our Years.* Privately printed, 1987.

Smith, Mae Trovillion. *The Zetetic and Socratic Literary Societies of Southern Illinois Normal University.* Carbondale, IL: University Publications Committee, 1949.

Stover, John F. *History of the Illinois Central Railroad.* New York: Macmillan Publishing Company, Inc., 1975.

Wright, Agnes Lentz, ed. *Carbondale Remembered.* Privately printed.

Wright, John W. D., *A History of Early Carbondale, Illinois.* Carbondale, IL: Southern Illinois University Press, 1977.

The Small Business Incubator. The newest building (on Pleasant Hill Road) opened in 1990. The function is to help new businesses in the area. The building, which is not in the traditional mode, cost six million dollars.

# INDEX

Abe Martin Baseball Field, 117
Ackerman, William K. 126
Adams, Tony 187
Agriculture Building, 65
Albon, George, 98, 122
Albon, Trix, 117
Alice Wright Day Care Center, 105
All American City, 65
Allen, John, 117
Allen, William J., 40, 112
Allyn Building 158, 191
Allyn, Robert, 38
Alpha Gamma Delta, 67
Alpha Phi Omega 179
Altgeld, John 190
American Legion, 116
American Pants Factory (Lerner-Sloane Clothing Corp.), 33
Amtrak, 128, 148
Amy Lewis Hospital, 32, 38, 112
Anderson, Dora, 116
Anderson, J. M., 5
Anderson, Joe, 102
Anderson, John O. 189
Andres, Esther, 180
Anthony Hall, 158,159, 160, 191
Archer, Eliabeth Lutz, 59
Archer, Richard, 184
Arena, 160, 189, 194
Armstrong, Cecil, 44
Armstrong, Delores, 180
Arnold, J. J., 81
Ashley, I.F., 10
Ashley, Lewis W., 10
Atherton, Oscar, 109
Ayer and Lord Tie Co., 12, 32, 127
Babcock, Edwin, 38
Backus, A. J., 5
Baggett, Gary, 95
Baggett, Les, 179
Baily, Percival, 189
Baird, Bill, 89
Banks—Bank of Carbondale, 98, 101
  Carbondale National, 32, 97, 98, 100
  First Bank, 98
  First National Bank and Trust, 11. 32. 44. 97, 98, 99
Barber, George F., 85
Barnes, Tom, 51
Barr, W. W., 97
Barrett, Troy, 78
Barrow, Alice, 104
Barrow, Mrs. J. W., 103, 104, 118
Barrow, Jack, 113
Barrow, James W., 38, 40, 104, 112, 113, 114
Barth Theater (Rogers), 49
Barton, John Harris, 54
Bass, Jewel 113
Batson's Livery and Boarding Stable, 12
Bellamy, John, 79
Beta Sigma Phi, 116
Beveridge, John L., 158
Black, George, 103
Bleyer, Bill, 184
Bleyer, Frank and Lita, 42
Bolen, Jim, 173
Boomer, Mrs. S.F., 118
Borkon, Eli, 113
Boudreau, Don, 173
Bowen Gym, 90, 94
Bowyer, Emma, 118
Brackett, Isaac P., 188
Braden, Clark, 89
Bradley, Mrs. G. L., 118
Brandon, W.A., 113
Brandt, Warren W., 161, 188
Brasfield, L.C., 95
Brewer, Fern, 102
Brewster, John, 10, 18
Bridges, Frank, 94, 109
Bridges, Ladaw, 119
Bridges, Harold E., 177
Brooks, Clyde 113
Brown, Glenn, 169, 189
Brown, James M., 188
Brown, Leo J., 17, 32, 38, 113, 114
Brown, Mary Barrow, 17, 104, 117
Brown, Rhoda Mae Baker, 48
Brown, W.O., 102
Brubaker, A.D., 102
Brubaker, Dora, 102
Brush, Bessie, 79
Brush, Charles, 19

Brush, Daniel Harmon, 8, 10, 11, 27, 80, 89
Brush, Frances and Rowland, 81
Brush Towers, 71
Bryan, William Jennings, 169
Bullard, S. A., 82
Bundy, Lillian, 118
Burket, J. H., 5
Caldwell, Andrew, 39
Caldwell, Delia, 80
Cameron, Mrs. D.H., 54
Campbell, George, 44
Campbell, Henry, 19, 97
Campbell, James G., 97
Campbell, James H, 89
Campbell, Ray, 103
Campus Lake, 185
Cannedy, Don, 115
Carbondale Business Men's Association, 33
Carbondale City Hall, 45
Carbondale City Panhellenic, 116
Carbondale Clinic, 113, 114, 115
Carbondale Garden Clubs, 116
Carbondale-Murphysboro Trolley, 49
Carbondale Park District, 104, 105, 109, 111
Carbondale Public Library, 86, 102, 103
Carbondale Woman's Club, 116
Carmen, Zeb, 113
Carpentier, Charles, 182
Carter's Cafe, 76
Cassell, William, 113
Catt, Harold, 50
Cavett, R. J., 126
Chaney, Martin, 76
Chapman, Carney, 189
Chapman, Frank, 82, 84
Charter Bank, 99
Cherry, Doug, 95
Cherry, John, 95
Chester Savings Bank, 99
Christopher, Elmer, 89
Churches—Bethel African Methodist Episcopal, 87
  First Baptist, 80, 82, 83
  First Christian, 80, 85
  First Methodist, (Old Blue) 11, 30, 80, 84, 112
  First Presbyterian, 80, 81, 89
  Grace Methodist, 84
  Olivet Free Will Baptist, 87
  Rock Hill Baptist, 87
  St. Andrew's Episcopal, 85, 102
  St. Francis Xavier, 21, 39, 86
  University Baptist, 83
  Walnut Street Baptist, 48, 83
CIPS, 47, 53
Cisne, Willis, 192
City Dairy, 33, 74, 78
Clemens, W., 97
Clements, Frank, 97
Colp Lumber, 127
Communications Building, 160
Compton, S.M., 101
Conner, Asgil, 10, 80, 81, 112
Cornstock, Fred, 89
Cox, William and Violet, 52
Cozad, Dale, 183
Crab Orchard Lake, 33, 104, 109
Craine, Carl, 9
Crandall, James H., 5
Crandle, Ellis, 113
Crane, Bob, 95
Crawshaw, Gene Paul, 94
Crim, Alonzo A., 87
Crowe, Jesse, 98
Crowell, Alice Hill, 174
Curd, Harlan, 38
Curtis, H. C., 5
*Daily Egyptian*, 159
Dairy Queen, 74
Daniels, Maude, 116, 118
Davenport, B. Haddon, 73
Davies Gymnasium, 68
Davis, I. Clark, 177
Davis, Lydia, 174
Davis, Midge, 48
Davis, Robert, 73, 98, 176
Delta Chi, 66
Delta Sigma Epsilon, 67
Delta Zeta, 66
Dempsey, Rey, 187
Derge, David R., 161, 188
Diamond, Mike, 103
Dickerman Building, 38
Dillinger, J. C., 77
Dillinger, J. M., 5
Dillinger, R. K., 181
Dillinger's Store, 77

Dixon, Claude, 32
Dixon, William C., 5
Dodillet, Imogene, 179
Doherty, Barbara, 117
Domer, Alan, 105
Dorsey, Diane, 117
Dorsey, May, 82
Doty, John, 79
Doughty, Almira, 81
Douglas Corps Cadets, 168
Douglas, Stephen A., 150
Doyle, Larry, 124
Duff, Andrew D., 16
Dunaway, Samuel W., 16, 20, 97
Duncan, Perry, 187
Dwyer, Leo I., 5
Dyer, Bill, 91
Eads, Albert (Mr & Mrs) 189
Eagles Club, 116
Easterly, Charles, 5, 44
Eckert, Neal E., 5
Edwardsville Campus, 160
Elks Club, 32, 116, 117, 120-121, 122
Ellis, Winifred, 79
Elmore, Dolph, 89
Emme Harold, 95
Entsminger, Dave, 89
Entsminger, Gilbert, 89
Entsminger, Mary, 189
Entsminger's, 61
Errett, Julia, 102
Etherton, Fred, 113
Etherton, Helen, 71
Etherton, J.E., 51, 71, 73, 100
Etherton, James M., 97, 98, 100
Etherton, Julia Mitchell, 23, 71, 116
Etherton, Monroe, 97, 100, 113
Etherton, William, 71, 98, 103
Evergreen Terrace, 160
Everest, Harvey W., 158, 162
Ewing, C. L., 97
Fair, Eugene R., 159, 163
Faner Hall, 68, 163, 172
Federer, Jane, 93
Feirich, Charles, 21
Feirich, Minnie, 117
Felts, William, 113
Ferrell, Hosea V., 101
Fichtel, Ernie, 117
Fichtel, Randall, 122
Fildes, Charles, 113
Fischer, Hans, 5, 123
Flagler, Samuel A., 5
Fluck, Ben, 89
Foley, Dan, 113
Foley, Jean Smith, 36, 48, 117, 119
Forde, Elvis, 187
Foster, Helen, 117
Fox, Ben, 113
Fox, Claude, 17, 38, 52
Frank Bleyer Football Field, 90
Frazier, Walt, 186
Freeburg, Ruth, 184
Frier, Susan, 51
Fritz, Dan, 179
Fry, Carroll, 5
Fulkerson, Mrs. Elbert, 118
Fuller, Buckminster, 185
Furr, Dorothy, 175
Furr, Paul, 189
Furr, William, 192
Gallatin, Harry, 187
Gallegly, Robert, 48
George Young Laundry, 49
Giant City State Park, 32, 104, 106, 107
Gilbert, Helen, 119
Gilbert, Jr., Dr., 73
Gilbert, Phil, 95
Gillett, Ben, 89
Gladders, Jean, 119
Gladson, Guy, (Mr & Mrs), 189
Goddard, Earl, 50
Goetz, Harry, 73
Goff, John, 103
Goforth, Benny, 173
Golliher, John Logan, 28
Good Luck Glove Co., 54
Good Samaritan Ministries, 84
Goodman, Benny, 173
Gorman, Ida and Dave, 76
Greathouse, Isodora, 28
*Green Diamond*, 146, 147
Green Mill Restaurant, 129
Greek Row, 160
Gregory, Dick, 178
Gregory, Roy, 134
Grief, Ransom, 87

Gross, Mrs. Chalmer, 118
Gubleman, Lilian, 79
Gullet, Ruby, 117
Gunn, Margaret, 175
Guyon, John C., 161, 188
Haile, Gene, 178
Hall, Hal, 175
Halloween Festival, 44
Hamilton, William, 39, 70
Hand, George H., 182
Hand, Randolph, 182
Hanes, Michael, 185
Hankla, Alma, 76
Harker, O.A., 11, 23, 97, 98
Harmon, Margaret, 37
Harriman, W. Averell, 148
Harrington, Lawrence, 21
Harris, Father W. John, 86
Hart, Jim, 181
Harwood, Samuel, 101
Harwood, Mrs. Samuel, 102
Hayes, Lillian, 119
Held, Fred, 44
Heritage Hills, 65
Hewitt, F. M., 17, 27, 100, 122
Hewitt, Will, 38
Hewitt's Drug Store, 113
Hickory Lodge, 109
Hill, Bert E., 5, 32
Hilton, Mina, 54
Hiskey, Marshall S., 177
Hoffner, Steven, 5
Holden Hospital, 40, 112, 113
Holmes, Gladys, 93
Home Culture Club, 32
Home Federal Savings & Loan, 99
Hooker, Mrs. A. F., 102
Hord, Thomas F., 5
Hotels—East Side, 12
  Edwards House, 12
  Hundley House (Prince), 12, 13, 29, 33, 129
  Newell House (Roberts), 12, 33, 76, 119
  Planters House (Franklin), 11, 12, 33, 49, 70, 134
  Southern Hotel, 12
  Union House, 70
Houghton, C. T., 54
House, Harry, 89
Howe, W.A., 109
Hub Cafe, 113
Huffman, G. R., 32,34, 35
Huffman, Nyle, 44, 117
Hull, John, 162
Hundley, J.C., 5, 11, 19, 20, 29, 98
Illinois Central Gulf, 143
Illinois Central Railroad, Chapter V
Illinois Department of Transportation, 78
Illinois Federation of Women's Clubs. 118
Illinois Fruit Growers, 127
Illinois State Health Laboratory, 33, 55
Independence Day, 10
Ingersoll, E. J., 5, 11, 15
Ingli, Donald A., 177
Inman, William B., 54
Ismert, Mildred, 117
IOOF, 116
Jaycees, 116, 124
Jackson Country Club, 105
Jennings, "Peanut", 91
Jim and Ruth's Market, 77
John, Jimmy, 173
Johnson, Charles, 5
Johnson, James M. 5
Johnson, Ralph, 186
Johnson, Rick, 187
Johnson's Dry Goods, 53
Johnson, Vancil, Taylor Co., 42, 43, 53
Johnston, Wayne, 127
Joyner, Clarence, 79
Joyner,. F. T., 97, 98
Kappa Alpha Psi, 67
Karraker, Guy (Mr & Mrs), 189
Keeley Institute, 32, 40, 112
Keene, Ada, 116
Keene, David, 5
Keller, Kent, 33
Kennedy, John F. 69
Kenney, David, 50, 51, 69, 102, 123
Kenney, Margaret, 51
Kenney, Ruth, 113
Kenney, Mrs. W. L., 81
Kettring, Eugene, 91
Kimmel, Barbara, 117
Kimmel, Mary Alice Brown, 117
Kimmel, Philip, 53

Kirk, Donald, 117
Kiwanis Club, 116, 117
Koonce, Harry, 127, 145
Koppers, 127
Kraatz, Karl (Mr & Mrs), 189
Kroger, 33, 62, 127
Krysher, F. C., 5
Lake Ridgeway, 160
Lambert, Guy W., 181
Lamer, William, 80
Landecker, Eva, 103
Langdon, Dick, 124
Langdon, Mrs. Tom, 118
Langdon, Tom, 54, 109, 111, 124
Lascer, Peaches, 95
Lauder, Hugh, 5, 81
Lawson, Douglas E., 193
Lawson, Tommy, 173
Lay, Chester F., 159, 163
Layer, Robert G., 161, 188
Lee, Arthur, 117
Legg, Glenn, 89
Lemma, William, 5
Lentz, Eli G., 16, 44, 158, 159
Lentz, Mrs. E. G., 118
Lesar, Hiram H., 161, 188, 193
Lethene, John, 112
Levelsmeier, Jerry, 123
Lewis, Elizabeth Harris, 33, 119
Lewis, John, Jr., 38, 54, 113
Lewis, John, Sr., 38, 98, 112
Lewis, Kenny, 95
Lewis, Roscoe, 38, 112
Liebig, Marilyn, 174
LIFE Community Center, 105
LIFE Science I, 182
Lightfoot, Richard, 16, 19
Lincoln, Abraham, 150
Lingle, Fred, 113
Lingle, Leland P., 189, 194
Lions Club, 116, 117
Logan, John A., 11, 14
Lopas, T. C., 80
Lottmann, Jerry W., 109
Louden, Cy, 89
Lutz, Betty Berry, 51, 59, 108
Lutz, Harry, 58, 59, 108
Lutz, Henry and Flaura, 58, 108, 118
Lynn, Bob, 91
Mackey, T. K., 101
Madison Square Garden, 186
Madrigal Singers, 180
Malone, Willis E., 177
Marberry, Bill, 105
Marberry, Charles, 50
Marberry, Jim, 50
Marching Salukis, 185
Mars, Mary, 110
Martin Baseball Field, 184
Martin, Glen "Abe", 184
Martin Oil, 127
Masons, 45, 116, 117
Masters, H. A. "Nick," 73
Maverick, Lewis A., 177
Maycock, Susan, 12, 32, 38, 39, 64, 65, 89, 126
McAnally, John T. and Mrs, 5, 17, 21, 97
McAnally, Merian, 21
McAndrew Stadium, 33, 111
McCadney, Farris, 180
McCammon, George E., 84
McCoy, Ralph, 102
McDaniel, Terry, 124
McDaniel, W. C., 177
McGrath, Robert, 179
McIntosh, Eva, 118
McLeod, Archibald, 193
McRoy, Ann, 76
McRoy, Paul, Jr., 76
McRoy, Paul, Sr., 76
Medlin, Edna, 119
Medlin, Trish, 117
Memorial Hospital, 113, 114, 115
Midland Hills, 105, 108
Miller, D. Blaney, 5
Miller, J. W., 101
Mimick, John, 79
Mitchell, Betty, 102, 103
Mitchell, E. E., 5, 11, 23, 97, 98, 101
Mitchell, H. C., 97
Mitchell, James E., 11, 98
Moake, John T., 105
Modern Woodmen, 30
Mofield, Tom, 98
Moody, W. M., 87
Moody's Opera House, 12, 79, 116
Moore, Walt, 95

Moose Club, 116
Moreland, Floyd, 173
Moreno, Bonnie, 117
Morris, Delyte, 64, 159, 161, 176-179, 181-183, 189, 192
Morris, Dorothy, 117, 176, 180, 189
Morris, James, 75
Morris Library, 182
Moss, C. H., 113
Muckelroy, Marvin, 122
Muckelroy, Renzo, 192
Mueller, Robert, 177
Mulkey, Isaac, 80, 85
Murrie, B. J., 54
Murrie, Mattie Lou, 54
National Guard Armory, 33, 45, 55
Neal, Virginia, 117
Neber Building, 113
Neckers Building, 160
Neely, Aileen, 10, 85
Neely, Julia, 195
Newman, Florence, 93
Newsome, Edmund, 126
Newspapers—*Carbondale Transcript*, 11
  *Times (New Era)*, 11, 12
  *Carbondale Observer*, 11
  *Carbondale Free Press*, 11, 12
  *Carbondale Democrat*, 11
  *Herald*, 32, 33, 44, 54
N.I.T., 160, 186
Nixon, Richard M., 183
Norfleet, B.F., 117
Norman, C. William, 5
North, Samuel E., 97
North, Thomas E.., 97
Oakdale Park, 110
*Obelisk*, (l936), 48, 159
O'Brien, Bill, 184
Odaniell, Robert, 123
Ogden, Marcus H., 97
Oglesby, Richard J., 158
Old Main, 116
Oldenhage and Fakes Saloon, 13, 29
Otteson, Willard, 100
Paine, Dorothy, 173
*Panama Limited*, 127, 147
Parkinson, Alice, 21
Parkinson, Daniel B., 17, 21
Parkinson, Mrs. D. B., 21
Parkinson Laboratory, 159, 191
Parkinson, Raymond, 21, 79
Parrish, Arthur, 30
Partlow, Geof, 95
Patten, Eustis, 17, 22, 27, 98
Patterson, Alice, 118
Patterson, Mrs. H. J., 118
Patterson, H. W., 102
Paul and Virginia, 161
Pease, James A. 97
Penrod, T., 89
PEO, 116
Perdue, Charles, 103
Perkins, Bill, 95
Peters, J. D., 97
Phelps, Lee, 119
Phillips, Lucy, 116
Phillips, W. H., 19
Porter, E. K., 5, 17, 28, 38
Porter, Margaret, 169
Potter, Rene, 117
Potts, Dewey, 74
Prickett, Frank A., 5, 11, 28, 97, 98
Pritchett, Mrs. Gilbert, 54
Producers Creamery, 33
Prosser, Don, 102
Prosser, Dorothy, 117
Prosser, Everett, 73
Pulley, Jane, 117
Pulliam Hall, 64
Pulliam, Roscoe, 159, 163, 192
Quigley, Eileen E., 159, 192
Ragsdale, Ted, 103
Rapp, Isaac, 38, 81, 82
Rathjen, Charles, 124
Rauch, Mel, 89
Reef, Mrs. E. W., 102, 103
Rehn Building, 160
Rehn, Henry J., 159, 163
Reid, Frances Dillinger, 44
Reid Martin Athletic Field, 90
Renfro, Charles D. M., I, 11
Renfro, Charles D. M., III, 44, 98
Renfro, Francis, 44
Restivo, Paul, 184
Richart, Eliza A., 89
Richart, James Boyle, 5
Richart, James Moody, 97

Richart, William, 10, 81
Ritz Cafe, 33, 74
Roberts, Lowell E., 189
Robinson, Marguerite, 117
Rogers Theater, 75
Roosevelt, Eleanor, 182
Rotary Club, 116, 117
Rowan, Ada, 76
Rude, Harry, 44
Rudmore, Wilda, 76
Ruffner, Ralph W., 188
Salter, John, 40, 112
Sanders, Mrs. E. R., 103
Sanders, Henry, 40
Sanders, Madge, 118
Schilpp, Madelon, 102, 103
Schneider, Alicia, 109
Schmidt, William R., 5
Schneider, Alicia, 109
Schnieder, William B., 177, 195
Schools—East Side (Attucks), 11, 87, 89, 91
  West Side (Brush), 11, 85, 89, 90, 91, 95
  Carbondale College, 89, 92
  Carbondale Community High School, 33, 90, 93, 95
  Glendale, 90
  Lakeland, 90
  Lewis, 90
  Lincoln, 11, 89, 92, 96
  Parrish, 90, 96
  Springmore, 90, 96
  Thomas, 90, 96
  Winkler, 90
Schuler, H. B., 97
Schutte, Roscoe, Sr., 42
Schwartz Building, 45
Schwartz, Sarah Kimmel, 24-25.
Schwartz, Tom, 5l
Schwartz, Walker, 46, 73, 98, 122
Schwartz, William (Gus), 11, 24-25, 97, 98
Schwegman, William, 5
Scott, Levi, 80
Searing, Anne E., 76
Searing, J. H., 5
Senior Citizens Center, 96
Shockey, Larry, 184
Shryock Auditorium, 32
Shryock, Burnett, 16
Shryock, Henry William, 159, 163, 190
Shurtleff College, 160
Sigma Pi, 187
Sigma Tau Gamma, 66
Simon, Mary Ellen Curd, 38, 117
Simond, Katie, 117
Sisk, Carlton, 5
SIU Credit Union, 99
Small Business Incubator, 197
Smith, Arthur M., 159
Smith, Clyde, 21, 39, 50, 85, 117
Smith, Danny, 178
Smith, Frances, 21, 50
Smith, Helen, 36, 50
Smith, Mary Powers, 36, 116, 117
Smith, Mr. and Mrs. G. W., 21, 39, 50
Smith, Mae T., 195
Smith, Russell Eugene, 50
Smith, T.B.F., 32, 168
Snyder, Ephram, 84
Socratic Society, 12, 116
Southern Illinois Hospital Corporation, 113
Southen Illinois Univ. Board of Trustees, 64
Spear Roger, 123
Special Olympics, 111
Spees, Emil, 66
Spiller, A. L. 102
Spiller, Elma, 175
Spiller, Nettie, 117
Spinning Wheel, 173
St. Louis Division Office, 126
Steagall, Mary, 102
Stein, Hilda A., 177
Stephens, Clarence, 188
Sternberg, Vernon, 189
Stevenson, Adlai E., 177
Stewart, Robert, 81
Stocks, Walter, 173
Stone House, 161
Stone, W. Clement & Jessie O., 194
Storme, Glenn W., 98
Stotlar, John and Constance, 44, 56-57, 79, 116
Stotlar, John W. (Bud) and Monte, 56-57, 91, 184

Stover, John F., 126, 127
Stratton, William G., 182, 183
Strohman, Dorothy, 119
Stroup, Archie, 42
Stroup, Tid, 119
Student Center, 160, 194
Sullivan, Georgia, 100
Swanson, Jon, 124
Swartz, Willis, 159, 163, 189
Swindell, Mary Marberry, 33, 103, 117
Taft, William Howard, 190
Talley, C. Horton, 177
Tanner, Lillian, 79
Taylor, Chuck, 95
Taylor, Jack, 113, 114
Taylor, Jerry, 119
Taylor, Mabel, 116
Taylor, Roscoe, 79
Teeter, Robert, 117
Temple, Jim, 77
Templeton, Amanda, 81
Tenney, Charles, 177, 189
Tenney, Maude, 117
Theta Xi, 67
Thompson, James, 185
Thompson Lake, 64, 104, 105, 159
Thompson Point, 159, 160, 195
Thorp, John R., 98
Thrailkill, Mrs. E. M., 118
Tower Road, 65
Townes, Bill, 50
Triangle Construction, 127
Truelove, Jewell, 103
Truman, Harry, 69
Tuck Industries, 62
Triegel, Elmer, 102, 103
Turley, Lenus, 87
Turley Park, 87, 109
Unger, Sandra, 181
Unitarian Fellowship, 102
University Drug Store, 67, 76
University Mall, 78
University Park, 64
U.S. Railroad Administration, 142
Vandeveer, W.W., 181, 189
Varsity Drug Store, 75
Varsity Theater, 33
Vaughn, Charlie, 187
Veterans of Foreign Wars, 116
Vicary, Benny, 73
Vocational Technical Institute, 159
Vogler, Don, 47, 103
Vogler, Dorothy, 117
Vogler, E. W. 32, 47
Vogler, E. W., Jr., 47
Waldron's Store, 62
Walker Funeral Home, 38
Walkup, Winton, 145
Wallace, Terry, 95
Walls, David, 95
Waltemate, Dorothy, 180
Ward, Mae, 44
Warren, Jane, 48
Warren, Lillian, 116
Wayne, Ralph, 76
Weaver, Mrs. T. A., 102
Westberg, Helen, 5
Wham Building, 160
Wheeler Library, 171, 190
White, Crillon E., 5
William McBride Learning Center, 90
Williams, Gwyneth, 173
Williams, John, 73
Williams, Julia and Thompson, 80
Williamson, Harry, 145
Wilson, Henry, 79
Winne, G. T., 19
Wiseman, Jonathan, 80
Wood, Josiah, 80, 81
Woodlawn Cemetery, 11, 15
Woods, Mrs. Clyde, 118
Woods, Brad, 95
Woody, Lucy K., 118
Woolard, Doug, 95
WPA, 55
Wright, Claude (Spider), 46, 73
Wright, Clarence, 98
Wright, Mrs. Jon I., 116
Wright, John I., 5, 46
Wright, John W. D., 11, 88, 112, 126
Wright, Mary, 117
Wykes, William, 97
Yellow Cab, 53
Young, Grace, 117
Young, W. O., 112
Zetetic Society, 12, 116

# First National
## Bank and Trust Company

**BOARD OF DIRECTORS**

Seated from left to right: William Budslick, Jr., (on couch arm), Kassy Simonds, Kathryn A. Schwartz and Charles D. Renfro. Seated back row: Joe R. Kesler. Standing back row: Geroge M. Twomey and Archie Stroup.